IF ONLY
YOU'D KNOWN
. . . you would have raised
so much more.

Also by Tom Ahern

What Your Donors Want . . . and Why!
The Ultimate Guide to Successful Fundraising
Communications, 171 pp., $24.95.

What Your Donors Want...and Why! debunks common myths and explores in depth the psychology and neuroscience behind loyal donors. It's written in Tom Ahern's easygoing jargon-free style, heavily illustrated with recent real-world examples from charities of all sizes.

Making Money with Donor Newsletters
The How-to Guide to Extraordinary Results, 166 pp., $24.95.

Making Money with Donor Newsletters will help you transform your current newsletter into a money machine -- some charities that have followed Tom's advice have improved income by 1000 percent! More importantly it will guide you in transforming your organization from a ho-hum 'corporate-focused' entity into a distinctive and thriving 'donor-focused' powerhouse.

Seeing Through a Donor's Eyes
How to Make a Persuasive Case for Everything from
Your Annual Drive to Your Planned Giving Program
to Your Capital Campaign, 167 pp., $24.95

Too many fundraisers – both verbally and in writing – fall flat when asked the question: Why should I support you? They stammer, equivocate, lapse into jargon – they do everything but make a convincing case for the would-be donor. If that describes you, then your capital campaign, annual drive, planned giving program, even your website is raising far less than it could if you adopted Tom's field-tested advice.

How to Write Fundraising Materials that Raise More Money
The Art, The Science, The Secrets, 187 pp., $24.95.

Do one small thing, and it's likely you can boost your gift income this year by 15 percent. Simply send out materials your donors actually *enjoy* reading. That's it. Really. It's easier than you think and it's exactly what Tom Ahern shows you how to do in his bestselling book, *How to Write Fundraising Materials that Raise More Money: The Art, the Science, the Secrets*.

www.emersonandchurch.com

IF ONLY
YOU'D KNOWN
. . . you would have raised so much more

Airtight Answers to 40 Questions
Essential to Your Fundraising Success

TOM AHERN

Emerson
& Church
PUBLISHERS

Emerson & Church, Publishers

Printed in the United States of America

This text is printed on acid-free paper.

Copies of this book are available from the publisher at discount when purchased in quantity.

Emerson & Church, Publishers
15 Brook Street, Medfield, MA 02052
Tel. 508-359-0019
www.emersonandchurch.com

ISBN 978-1-889102-71-9

Library of Congress Cataloging-in-Publication Data Pending

Dedication

To the truest of true believers; hearts like the ones you sewed
to your sleeves, Simone, as a determined child with glasses

"The code is more what you'd call 'guidelines' than actual rules."

—Captain Hector Barbossa, *Pirates of the Caribbean*

He's explaining the real-life limits of the Pirate's Code.

It's the same for donor communications work.
Once you learn the rules, feel absolutely free to break them.
I do, with glee, every working day.

Contents

The moment

A recollection and exhortation

by Simone Joyaux, ACFRE, Adv Dip

I'm quietly working in my office.
Haven't seen the life partner yet; that would be Tom Ahern, by the way.

Suddenly, quiet no longer.

Thud. Thud. Thud. His footsteps coming down the stairs.

Walking purposefully into my office.

His first words: "I don't know how the hell you people have ever raised any money."

My response: "Good morning, Tom. How are you? So which 'you people' are we talking about?"

"You fundraisers."

And he proceeds: "I'm looking at hundreds of pieces of donor communications per year—and most of it stinks."

Now you've met the author of this book.

So here I am. And here you are.

Let's start with why nonprofit stuff stinks.

Because your boss and board members don't let you do it right, maybe? Maybe because you don't yet know *how* to do it right.

Fundraising is tough. It's huge. It's complicated. It's very counterintuitive. But, hey, it's your job to learn that immense body of knowledge, to follow research, to copy best practice—and to apply all that inside your own organization.

It won't be easy.

I promise you: you're going to have to fight your boss, your colleagues, board members, and maybe even the file drawer in the corner. And you'll likely have to do this fighting (and managing) forever.

Here's the thing: Most fundraising problems are not really fundraising problems. They're organizational culture problems. And too often, they are "merely" dumb power problems, as well. ("I'm the CEO of that big company . . . and I know more than you do, Missy.")

Oh ye fundraisers, get ready for the real world!

At the same time as you are learning the fundraising body of knowledge, you will need to learn other stuff like:

- How to shepherd organizational development

- How to build a culture of philanthropy

- How to insist on good governance (the board tends to trespass)

- How to manage up and how to manage conflict

- And more . . .

Sure, this is a fundraising book.

Just remember that going-from-good-to-great in fundraising requires knowledge of so many things *other* than fundraising.

The sky's the limit.

You're the one.

The Ignorance Ceiling: Why this book screamed to be made

This book is not for my professional friends and colleagues. They already know most of this stuff.

This is for everyone who hopes and prays their nonprofit will change the world . . . but *doesn't* know this stuff.

In the US, as of 2017, there were something like 1.3 million government-sanctioned charitable organizations. It's a growing sector: at current rates, about 47,000 new US charities are born each year.

Is that a lot or a little, for a nation of some 330 million?

I say it's a lot. The same population of mouths gets by with just 190,000 licensed dentists.

In the US, the nonprofit sector has become the third largest employer, after retail and manufacturing. It's a massive enterprise . . . and not *just* in America: the world is a hurting place.

Sympathetic governments do what they can afford or have the political will to do. But it's not nearly enough. In an attempt to cope, the nonprofit sector has grown across the globe, with accelerating momentum.

Yet, as an industry, we lack consensus on some basic stuff. And it's hurting our viability.

You see, amongst those 1.3 million US charities mentioned above lurk probably 20 million *disagreeing* opinions about how to do fundraising "the right way"—when you add up fundraisers, their bosses, their boards and assorted second-guessers (*program staff, I'm looking at you*).

That's just wrong. Not to mention counterproductive. And wasteful. And a great way to leave a lot of money on the table, hence starving the mission.

This book aims to break through the Ignorance Ceiling.

What's the #1 complaint I hear from fundraisers worldwide?

"I'd love to. But my boss says no!" As in, "I understand we need to tell stories. But my boss insists we focus on statistics instead." If I've heard it once, I've heard it a hundred times.

Here is the simple truth: the charity world suffers from an abundance of opinion . . . and a scarcity of knowledge at the approval/senior/C-suite level.

For example, executive directors and board chairs who've never had to raise a penny through direct mail blithely pass judgment on direct mail. "I'd never read a four-page letter!" they declare. And other flagrant acts of hubris. Confident. Unchallenged.

Every board member hopes to emerge a hero, saving the day with a bright idea and a strong opinion. They're not *trying* to be counterproductive, bless their hearts. But they are. Worst is the damage their ignorance does internally, by demoralizing their frontline fundraisers.

According to the dismal "Underdeveloped" report issued in 2013, 50 percent of fundraisers want a new employer, and 50 percent of employers want a new fundraiser. What the heck!?!

Let's get serious, people.

The book you hold in your hands offers fundraisers—and their overseers—a quick review of *some* of what's known—though maybe not yet *universally* known—about raising money, whether in-person, through your communications, or online.

World-class, best-in-industry fundraising practitioners generously provided the answers . . . from seven countries.

Of course, this won't answer every question. But it answers enough important, basic, essential, undeniable, worthwhile, profitable questions to demonstrate whether, in fact, your organization *already* knows it stuff . . . or could raise more money by adopting different ways.

Who are you talking to, *really?*

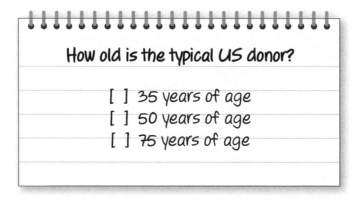

How old is the typical US donor?

[ ] 35 years of age
[ ] 50 years of age
[ ] 75 years of age

"A young donor in the US is sixty," expert Jeff Brooks noted in 2013. He shared the pie chart below. It breaks down giving in the US by age. How good is the data, you ask? It doesn't get any better: it comes from Target Analytics Group, a Blackbaud company. In 2019, Blackbaud managed the donor records for more than 28,000 charities in the US, Canada, Australia and the UK. It holds and deeply analyzes oceans of information about giving.

Is it different for your charity? "It comes out this way no matter who does the research," Jeff told me. "I've seen it many times through the years."

Donors aged sixty-five and older comprise (by far) the largest slice of the American charity pie. Those under age thirty-five comprised the smallest slice of the same pie.

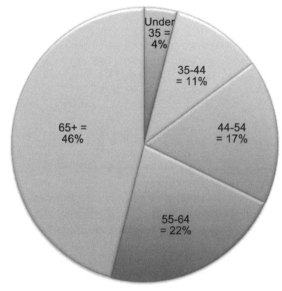

Under 35 = 4%

35-44 = 11%

44-54 = 17%

65+ = 46%

55-64 = 22%

Ages of Typical US Donors

What's typical? I know an animal rescue charity that acquired a new annual donor at age 55. She sent in her last donation at age 101, just before she died. The only thing unusual about that? Most of your donors won't stick around for forty-six years.

OK, but that's puppies and kittens. What about *other* kinds of charities? Are their donors *also* older?

For more than a decade, I've written direct mail appeals for a community hospital system in southern California. Tens of thousands of grateful ex-patients (i.e., the ones not suing) have chosen to become donors.

What's *their* average age? Not seventy-four. Nor seventy-six. *Exactly* seventy-five years old. Accurate? We know to the day when EX-patients-who-then-become-donors were born: the information is in their medical records.

So, again, OK: puppies, kittens; hospitals curing people. What about a charity *without* these advantages: what's the "age profile" there?

In 2017, one of America's top 10 brand-name charities, a group serving the homeless and addicted, analyzed its vast donor database by age. Its *largest* group of "active" (i.e., repeat) donors was eighty-seven years old **on average**. Its largest group of *first-time* (i.e., new) donors was age seventy **on average**.

Even in Australia, a philanthropic market that vigorously courts younger donors, older donors end up ruling the roost. Sean Triner, co-founder of Pareto, that country's largest direct mail and phone fundraising agency, ran the numbers. He simply concluded: "Older donors are better."

Why? They tend to stick longer and hence give more in total.

But all that said, here's what Roger Craver, one of our planet's best-informed fundraising experts, thinks of the "age debate":

> Looking at Millennials with the belief they act one way or the other as a group is not reliable. In fact, it's probably better to look at any other factor than age to get an idea of a person's likelihood to contribute.

When and why people start giving

Are younger Americans less generous? Not at all. But they lack one essential: money to give away.

Young adults are building lives. They're buying stuff. They're forming and furnishing households. They are as caring and concerned and compassionate as anyone else. But unless they were born with the proverbial silver spoon, they probably don't have all that much disposable income to throw around (especially if they choose to have children, an expensive proposition in America).

And then things change.

"At age fifty-five" Jeff Brooks observed, "people start to become reliably charitable. They're starting to have some extra money." There is some surplus in their wallets: the kids are launched, the house is almost paid for. "*Then* households begin giving to charity," said Jeff. "And their giving ramps up until age sixty-five, where it levels off. They'll continue giving until something intervenes." They get ill. They grow destitute. They die.

It's tempting to romanticize the act of giving. We admire generosity. It's a positive trait, the sign of a "good" person. But circumstances have to be right. People give to charity because they have disposable income . . . and because something a charity said caught their eye and moved them.

Did I give your nonprofit $30? That's because I think I *can* give away $30 at this particular time . . . without changing my lifestyle one bit. I sacrificed *nothing* (maybe a couple of lattes). Many gifts to charity are impulse purchases, the same purchases that fill your closets and drawers.

Who are donors, really? Serial entrepreneur Seth Godin offered this sobering insight: target markets (such as prospective donors) are often "lazy people in a hurry." Keep your expectations in check.

Are major gifts different? What if someone gave you $30 million instead of $30?

To the charity, the gift is massive, maybe transformational. Yet it probably didn't alter the donor's lifestyle in the least. Still have the summer place on Martha's Vineyard. Still have the plastic flamingos on the lawn (annoying the neighbors). Still have the gardener and pool crew to keep the place looking spiffy. Still have the top-notch financial advisors growing my fortune every year without fail.

A $30 million gift won't necessarily be an *impulse* gift . . . but it's unlikely to be a sacrifice, either.

When you say "younger" donors, what do you mean exactly?

"The younger [youngest] groups will NOT stay with you in good numbers," Jeff Brooks noted, "even if you can find them.

"But the 'almost old' are promising. They give higher average gifts than sixty-five-plus, and once they're aboard, they can stay with you for many years. This is the group that can turn around your fortunes and drive you to a brighter future."

The next big "giving generation" will be baby boomers, born between 1946 and 1964. In 2018, the oldest were seventy-two, and the youngest were fifty-four. You won't see the last of them until 2064 or so. It's a rich river to fish in. Together, baby boomers control over 80 percent of personal financial assets in the US, says a well-sourced Wikipedia article.

CHAPTER 2

The eyes have it

So, for e
good cu

How big should the type be?

[ ] 10 pt.
[ ] 12 pt.
[ ] 14 pt.

"We need younger donors!"

No, you don't. They're nice to have, of course; the more support, the better. But younger donors will not magically solve your charity's financial problems.

As Stephen Stills sang in 1970, "Love the one you're with." Your best and most likely donors are older, as noted in the previous chapter. Read that fact again. You think you're speaking to *everyone* . . . but *in fact* you're mostly speaking to *older* folks.

Knowing that for a fact has consequences.

Around 2012, the AIGA (essentially, the graphics artists' trade group in the US) issued an advisory: "For eyes over 60, use 14-point type for body copy." This piece of advice is science based. It's the recommendation of agencies serving the vision-impaired.

Please understand: a good "customer-service experience" is the *chief* reason why donors stick with you, according to alpha-researcher Dr. Adrian Sargeant.

yes "of a certain age," 14 point type will be a *decently* ...tomer service experience . . . and 12 point type will *not* be.

- This sentence is set in 18 point type. Eyes aged sixty-five and older will love it.

- This sentence is set in 14 point type. Eyes aged sixty-five and older find it tolerable.

- This sentence is set in 12 point type. Eyes aged sixty-five and older find it barely readable. People who don't need corrective lenses love it.

- This sentence is set in 10 point type. Eyes aged sixty-five and older hate you. Younger eyes mostly ignore the inconvenience.

CHAPTER 3

Life review

People over seventy are still developing.

[ ] True
[ ] False

According to David Solie, geriatric psychologist, elderly people are on "a journey" unrecognized by most others, including their children and professional caregivers.

Unrecognized is the part that breaks my heart. "Many of us look at members of our parents' generation and see a diminished version of the vibrant people we once knew," he writes in his book, *How to Say It to Seniors*. "Surely they aren't developing anymore, because we can see them declining right before our eyes."

But that's not true.

They *are* developing . . . just NOT in the direction we expected. "Seniors" work their way daily through what Solie calls "their end-of-life tasks."

These tasks include "searching for a legacy." Solie also calls it "life review." It is essential and involuntary. "Every day, every hour, whether they mention it or not, the seventy-plus age group is reviewing their lives."

I bring this up because it's a stage of life unsuspected . . . until you get there. (*I'm there!*)

Acts of charity help define us as we age. They help define us *to ourselves*.

Acts of kindness say, "This is who I am, in part. On my best days, this is what I do for others. This is how I've tried to help. Much of life is selfish; it has to be, doesn't it? for survival and comfort. But this is me at my LEAST selfish."

The third act

London-based researcher Richard Radcliffe knows a lot about donors. He's quizzed more than 25,000 of them in focus groups, digging into why they give; he's been at it for decades.

In 2018, Richard made this frank observation about his own aging process:

> Never ever before have I had any will power—for decades I have been weak willed. I have always enjoyed my food and drink far too much and in the past had a few other typical addictions too. The same applies to my four older brothers. And my late Mum . . .

But just before Christmas, Radcliffe discovered a new depth of will power.

> I became fascinated in what made me change, in a second, to give up or reduce my intake of so many loves.

> After researching the world of older people (again) I discovered it was *me* being in the "Third Act" (of my life).

Intrigued now, Radcliffe wanted to know how the Three Acts of life apply to donors.

> The First Act is our first 30 years and perhaps a time when our donor instincts are ignited in school or by a family experience and taking part in sponsored events. There is empathy and energy but lack of commitment.

The Second Act, Radcliffe discovered:

> is when we are aged 30–60—a time of spontaneous empathetic response, but our lives are busy. So there is little time to research the performance and impact of our charities or even to read communications in any detail. Engagement is low only because of lack of time to engage. We are too busy building careers, starting families and later on possibly looking after older family members.

The Third Act is when we reach our "generosity peak."

> The Third Act [arrives] usually over the age of 60—which is when our minds and attitudes change vastly. There are elements which [characterize] the start and development of the Third Act:

- To finish life well

- Wisdom (in decision making)

- Completion (of all the things you have been meaning to do)

The evolutionary science behind charity

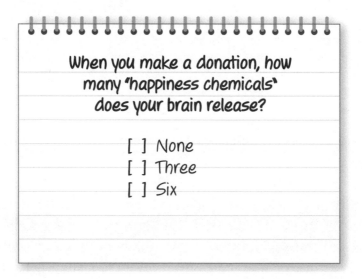

When you make a donation, how many "happiness chemicals" does your brain release?

[ ] None
[ ] Three
[ ] Six

"Giver's glow."

That's what Dr. Stephen G. Post calls it. He's director of the Center for Medical Humanities, Compassionate Care and Bioethics at New York's Stony Brook University. He's also the best-selling author of *Why Good Things Happen to Good People* and a distinguished researcher who's published more than three hundred peer-reviewed articles in places such as the *New England Journal of Medicine*.

As Post noted to reporter Elizabeth Renter, the act of giving "doles out several different happiness chemicals. These include dopamine, endorphins that give people a sense of euphoria, and

Why *do* people give? These quotes were lifted from a 2018 survey of "core" donors—the people who give regularly, if not always a lot. Ireland's top fundraising agency, Ask Direct, in cooperation with Bluefrog Fundraising, one of the UK's leading agencies, conducted the survey, published in November 2018 in an AskDirect blog post written by Caoileann Appleby.

oxytocin, which is associated with tranquility, serenity or inner peace."

Her 2015 *US News and World Report* article further explains: "This pleasure and reward system evolved some 1 to 2 billion years ago, and at its most basic level, is tied to the joy we receive from eating, sex and social interactions. Viewing the brain with MRI technology during moments of generosity or selfless behavior has led scientists to uncover that even the thought of giving can engage this ancient response."

CHAPTER 5

"You *are* that good!"

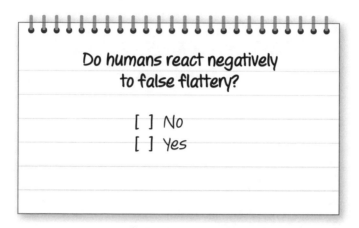

Do humans react negatively
to false flattery?

[ ] No
[ ] Yes

"Flattery will get you nowhere!"

Sounds right, right? In a rational world, flattery *would* get you nowhere . . . in fact, flattery might even be seen as the last resort of scoundrels.

Except our brains aren't really all that rational.

"Mom was wrong," Roger Dooley says in his book, *Brainfluence*. "Research shows that even when people perceive that flattery is insincere, that flattery can still leave a lasting and positive impression of the flatterer."

Of course, since I teach this stuff, I'm immune. I *know* when I'm being falsely flattered.

Correction: no, I don't. I fall for it every time.

As neuroscience has now determined, the human brain didn't evolve to discern between true flattery and false flattery. *All* flattery makes us feel good.

Which leads to this wonderful corollary: You cannot tell your donors too often how wonderful they are. With flattery, the sky's the limit. This is a great power. Use it wisely.

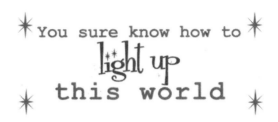

Dear Tom,

Pssst. Have you heard?

YOU'RE exceedingly extraordinary!

(Go ahead. Say that last sentence out loud. Again. And again!)

The enclosed newsletter shows you what a difference YOU'RE MAKING for 11-year-old Esther.

Before you came into her life, Esther was the victim of horrible cruelty.

But now, **you've come to her rescue, Tom.**

I love hearing from Vida Joven. Why? Because they make me feel great about my giving (and myself!) . . . over and over and over and over. This is the opening of a two-page cover letter included with the October 2018 print donor newsletter.

CHAPTER 6

You'll need a donor acquisition program

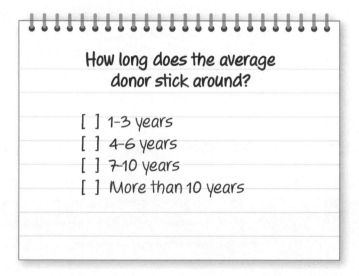

How long does the average
donor stick around?

[ ] 1-3 years
[ ] 4-6 years
[ ] 7-10 years
[ ] More than 10 years

Attrition's murder. But I didn't know just how bad. So I asked a simplistic question of colleagues who are far more experienced: "How long, do you think, the average donor gives to the same charity? 5 years? 10 years? 25 years? *Off the top of your head.*"

I didn't need three-decimal accuracy. I needed a rule of thumb.

Of course, these *were* some of the world's most successful, most compulsively analytical professionals. Their agencies work with hundreds of nonprofit clients across seven countries. So there was a good deal of throat-clearing and reservations. But they reached a consensus. . . .

Over half of first-time donors give just once, several respondents pointed out. Years of data collected in the US show that 70–80 percent of first-time donors will not—NOT!—give you a second donation.

Very few donors stay longer than a few years: precisely 4.6 years in the UK, according to Dr. Adrian Sargeant's research, based on an analysis of 5 million records. "It's an amalgam of all forms of giving, so it lumps together very different types of giving," he admitted. "But as a number, it's nice. And it's getting lower each year."

Which means: don't overestimate the "stickiness" of new donors. They quit quickly. A program for regularly acquiring new donors remains vital to your nonprofit's financial health.

Are they *intimately* connected or *casually*?

Beth Ann Locke said this: "The rise of peer-to-peer giving"—e.g., I sponsor you in a 10K run—"shortens the lifespan of donors. They give to a 'charity' but are really usually only giving to their friends. This certainly has the great opportunity of casting a wide net, but the net is gossamer."

Beth Ann is a veteran of major institutions.

Late in 2018, she became the chief development officer for the British Columbia Hospital and Health Centre (Vancouver). Before that she was director of advancement for one of the faculties at Simon Fraser University. Before that was another university. Before that was another healthcare organization.

Recall Beth Ann's comment as you read Mark Phillips' response (he's the founder and manager of Bluefrog in London, among the UK's most successful and lauded fundraising agencies): "I find that the best 5% of the file tend to stick with you forever. The problem is the other 70% of people who only ever intended to give once. They really drag your average down."

Roger Craver, author of *Retention Fundraising* and one of America's all-time direct mail champs, estimated donors stick around "about 4 to 5 years, top of my head. The single donors who only ever give one gift weigh down longevity [as Mark said]. If you're looking only at donors who make two or more gifts [for instance, monthly donors], I would say the span is closer to 7 or 8 years."

P.O. BOX 510167
St.Louis MO, 63151 USA

CRISIS AID
INTERNATIONAL

November 7, 2018

Tom and Simone Ahern
10 Johnson Road
Foster, Rhode Island 02825-1230

Dear Tom,

WOW! Can you believe that you have been a part of the Crisis Aid family since 2006? **What an incredible testament of <u>WHO YOU ARE</u> and what you have done** for so many. Thank you for your partnership and for all you have done!

It seems like just yesterday we were starting off with a 2-pound bag of rice, determined to do more than just watch as people literally starve to death. **You took up that challenge with us,** and look where we are today – *over 2.4 million people served worldwide*! <u>And all because of YOU!</u>

The dream does not stop here. It continues to grow and to expand far beyond today. It reaches into the lives of these precious people for years to come. We are determined to help the people of East Africa make a permanent "life-giving" change for themselves and their families. Our goal is to provide them with opportunities they never had.

THE NEED:

As you know, **abject poverty** consumes the eastern region of Africa where we work. We see it every day; children literally starving to death right before our very eyes. This was the cruel reality we saw when we first met Asha. Her death from starvation broke something in us, and the phrase **"refuse to do nothing"** took on a stronger, more urgent meaning. We

One way to keep donors giving year after year? Make a glorious deal of their anniversary, as Crisis Aid's letter did with me. As a donor to many causes, I can attest that being reminded of when my anniversary gift is due is a welcome reminder (*because I forget*). I have one critique. The Crisis Aid envelope teaser was generic: "No child should ever be left to die from starvation!" I didn't know from the envelope that this was MY anniversary reminder, so I might easily have thrown it away. Get serious: most of us ignore most of our direct mail most of the time.

Nor are all charities and events equally compelling.

"When I had my heart attack, my local hospital fixed me right up!" Now that's an event to remember. I'll tell everyone willing to listen.

Spending an entertaining evening at the theater? Nice, of course; but will you remember it and be grateful for the rest of your life? Will you influence them?

Yours *forever?*

Rory Green, associate director of advancement, Faculty of Applied Sciences, Simon Fraser University: "Many of my donors have given consecutively for 10+ years . . . BUT we're a bit of an anomaly. I would imagine the answer would differ, too, across generations: [older people] longer and less so as donors get younger."

Beth Ann Locke agreed: "I think older donors are more loyal. [At one hospital, there were] donors who had had hips and knees replaced who just gave and gave, as long as you kept asking, for 20+ years. I'd say with some universities it is the same, once the habit takes hold."

In contrast, Beth Ann saw a different pattern when she raised money for an art museum: "You would bring them into the fold as donors after being members. Then they would fall off in a few years."

What does that tell us? I don't know.

Maybe it just means that people lose interest.

I know I do. I imagine you do, too.

CHAPTER 7

Overwhelming

How quickly should you thank
a first-time donor?

[ ] Within forty-eight hours
[ ] Within a week
[ ] Within a month

W e're not talking about the automatic thank-you a robot generates when someone makes a gift online. That thanks takes a moment.

What we're talking about here is a truly personal thank-you—one sent person to person, not robot to person.

In 2011, Damian O'Broin, founder and manager of Ask Direct in Ireland, made a presentation in the Netherlands. He shared some startling research from McConkey Johnston International UK (now the Christian Fundraising Consultancy).

The research found that first-time donors who received a personal thank you within forty-eight hours were four times more likely to give again.

Yes: thanking in forty-eight hours = 400 percent improvement in renewal rates.

First-time donors are ardent. But that ardor cools fast if you don't sustain it. It's like a campfire ignited from tinder. You nurse it. You feed it oxygen, blowing across it.

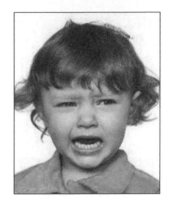

A super-quick personal thanks does the same: it blows oxygen across an ardent new donor, keeping that small flame alive, excited by your mission. At the very least, a super-quick personal thanks gets your organization past what often happens in the same forty-eight-hour period: buyer's remorse.

Look, the standard for thanking in the nonprofit world has fallen so low that *any* unusual gratitude on your part will probably net you far more friends. As The Agitator reported in 2013, "A three-minute thank-you phone call will boost first-year [donor] retention by 30%."

The ghastly truth is that most charities thank poorly (if at all). They predictably, relentlessly, remorsefully and (let's hope) unwittingly, UNDERwhelm their donors.

If you doubt that's the case, give small gifts to a handful of new-to-you charities and see for yourself.

Or, even easier, follow The Whiny Donor on Twitter. She describes herself this way: "On the development committees of two non-profits, and a donor to many others. Here I tell you what bugs me in the world of fundraising." Here are some of her recent tweets, all within a month:

- "When a local nonprofit uses fake handwriting on the envelope and appeal and mails it from a zip code far, far away . . . it feels neither personal nor local."

- "I've received no confirmation of my reservation to your special event, and you haven't cashed the check I mailed more than two weeks ago—which included an extra donation—so I sure hope you're expecting me."

- "Nowhere does it invite me to give online; the web address—or any other information—is nowhere to be found."

- "There's a box to check to waive all benefits so I can deduct the full amount of the donation for tax purposes, but there's no explanation of what those benefits are."

Dear Tom and Simone,

THANK YOU! Your generosity helped young Roza begin a new life!

When she first came to us, she was broken. Her life was a living nightmare and she no longer had dreams or hopes. She just survived in one of the worst Red Light districts on earth.

But slowly step by step, Roza began to dream again and she soon participated in Crisis Aid's vocational training program through Mercy Chapel – a church, counseling center and vocational training center. This center is designed to help girls like Roza receive counseling and learn a vocation to a better life.

However, this was never meant to be the "end" of the story, but rather the "beginning". And that was where YOU CAME IN!

Through your gift and other gifts like yours, Roza was able to move into her very own apartment! Together you provided her with basic furniture, kitchen utensils, the first three months of rent, and so much more.

And because you invested in her, she was able to put her past behind her and is now starting her own business; working with computers which is something she LOVES! Can you imagine what an unbelievable blessing that was for Roza when she learned what you had done for her?

On behalf of Roza, we say THANK YOU! And we celebrate with you, her new life and her new dreams.

God bless you,

Pat & Sue Bradley

Meet Roza
Vocational Training: Basic Computer
Current Status: Starting her own Business

I've been giving to Crisis Aid for more than a decade. They are some of the best "thankers" I know. Everything they send me makes me feel better about myself and the world.

- "Got an unsegmented appeal from an org we've donated to consecutively for close to twenty years. Kind of like your own aunt not recognizing you."

If I could only give any charity one small piece of advice, it would be this: don't be hopelessly lousy at thanking.

Be the "OVERwhelmer" instead. You *will* reap rich rewards. I *guarantee* you will reap rich rewards. Neuroscience says so. The accumulated experience of the world's top fundraisers says so. The Whiny Donor says so. And I, as a frequent donor, say so.

Nostalgia can be a powerful driver in alumni fundraising. Michigan State University thanks major donors with useful surprises such as these notecards, illustrated with watercolors of campus landmarks.

CHAPTER 8

More thanks = more money

Should you include an "ask"
in your thank-you letter?

[ ] Always
[ ] Never
[ ] Dealer's choice

Lisa Sargent is an internationally recognized expert on thanking. And she says, as a rule, "Never, ever, include an ask in a thank you. And never, ever, include a donation reply slip." She also notes, however, "I reserve the right to change my mind based on results."

Jeff Brooks has had different results. "We've found," he wrote in 2014, "that it's BEST to include a reply coupon in receipts (plus a return envelope). It dramatically increases response, which leads to better retention. The thing NOT to do is use standard ask techniques, like sad stories, negative photos, urgency, etc. The tenor of the package must be thankfulness and good news. The ask is just 'My next gift.' You're talking to someone who really gets it, and is emotionally well positioned to give again."

Lisa continues to test her "never" premise, but so far it's held up with her clients. One client does add a Business Reply Envelope to every thank-you, as a convenience if someone wishes to send a check. But there is no reply device with the envelope, nor does the thank-you letter ask for a gift.

Guidelines, not rules

Like Lisa, keep an open mind. Angel Aloma, executive director at Food for the Poor, reports, "On average, we get more than one-fifth of our net income from direct mail from our thank you letters." Like Lisa, he doesn't make an ask in these letters, but he does include an envelope and a reply device.

In 2012, Angel ran a test with 50,000 of that charity's top donors:

On November 6, 2018, Julie Capaldi, executive director at the United Way of Pickens County, reported, "I am now on my 50th handwritten thank-you note to $1,000+ donors." Other US United Ways report declining revenues. In Pickens County, South Carolina, despite a low median household income, giving to the United Way has grown 20 percent in three years, thanks in part to Julie's persistent focus on gratitude and donor-centricity.

- 25,000 received an extra thank-you at the beginning of the year. This mailing was a simple expression of gratitude for past generosity. There was no ask or reply device included.

- 25,000 did NOT receive this extra thanks.

Twelve months later, Angel reviewed the results.

Both groups had given the same number of gifts. But, tantalizingly, the group that received the extra thank-you note was more generous. That group gave almost $450,000 more in total during the year than the group that did not receive the extra thank-you.

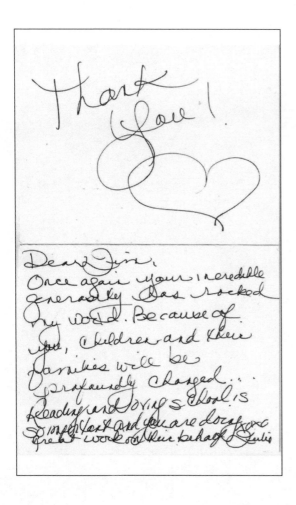

CHAPTER 9

Don't fall for your own nonsense

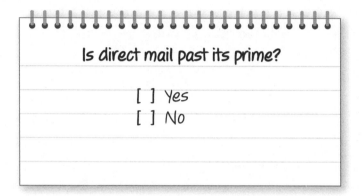

Is direct mail past its prime?

[ ] Yes
[ ] No

For a couple of decades, fundraising futurists have droned on about the impending demise of direct mail, deeming it doomed and irrelevant in an increasingly digital age.

And it's not just in fundraising. The same fears haunt the commercial world. As *Forbes* magazine reported in August 2017, "One of the biggest urban legends is: Direct mail is dead. It was killed by the internet. However, it's not just alive and well, but in fact, direct mail could be considered superior to other marketing channels based on recent statistics and studies. . . . [D]irect mail's response rates are actually anywhere from 10 to 30 times higher than that of digital."

As Mark Twain wrote a worried friend, "The report of my death was an exaggeration."

- Fact (not opinion) #1: Direct mail is still **by far** the way most US charities, big and small, attract new, first-time, "first date" donors.

- Fact (not opinion) #2: Direct mail is how most US charities successfully ask their current donors to give yet again. . . . NOT via email (which recipients ignore, by and large) . . . but via direct, physical, well-personalized, non-boring direct mail. (Phone calls are a big help, too.)

Direct mail, in fact, drives a lot of online giving.

Jeff Brooks noted in 2014: "Direct mail sends more people to give online than any digital medium like Facebook or email does." Boston-based expert Tina Cincotti said that 15 percent to 37 percent of online gifts she sees are prompted by a letter. "Plus," she cautions, "donors are three times more likely to give online in response to a direct mail appeal than to an email appeal.

"Direct mail not only isn't dead. It's more important than ever."

Tina makes another point, this time about multiple touches.

"By receiving a letter and then giving online, that supporter has become worth more to you. Donors connected to you through multiple [touch] points give at least 20% more than donors connected through only one channel. They also have better conversion rates [shifting to monthly giving, increasing their average gifts]. And higher retention rates.

"So you'd best be fundraising *both* online *and* offline."

The danger . . . and where the real money hides

One clear danger to direct mail fundraising is the ever-rising cost of postage.

As Patricia Vidov of Operation Smile Canada pointed out in 2015, "There's nothing like the mail to tell your story. But it's expensive. . . . You have to spend 50-plus cents to get it to them, then another 75 cents to get their gift back and another 75 cents to thank them."

The outbound expense is the killer.

If the response rate to your direct mail acquisition appeal is 1 percent (which counts these days as a reasonable return for a non-premium direct mail pack), then 99 percent of your mailing has produced zero revenue.

That's a lot of printing and postage expended to land one new donor. An oft-heard rule of thumb is, "In acquisition, you'll spend two dollars to raise a dollar." You'll spend $60 to land a $30 gift.

You only go into the black on direct mail when *and if* that newly acquired donor gives again and again. Too few do: as noted before, eight out of ten first-time donors in the US, on average, do not make a second gift to the same charity.

So: while acquiring new donors is vitally important to refresh and grow your base, your skill at *retaining* those new donors is where the real money hides. And what are the key "retention skills" you'll need? Become adept at using "donor-centricity" in your thanks and reporting (see chapter 35).

The 100% Fallacy

What's a successful response rate
for a donor-acquisition appeal?

[ ] 15% (you mail 100, you get fifteen
gifts back)

[ ] 8% (you mail 100, you get eight gifts
back)

[ ] 1% (you mail 100, you get one gift back)

L et's pretend.

Let's pretend you are sending out a direct mail appeal. You have great hopes. In fact, you *need* to attract a bunch of new donors. Otherwise, as you're aware, perfectly normal attrition will knock your fundraising program on its ass.

You're pumped!

You have the *perfect* mailing list. (We're pretending here.)

Every name on your rented list is pre-qualified. They all actually live where the addresses says they live. They really *do* care about your cause. How do you know?

Because they *already* give or gave to a similar cause.

I.e., you're a conservation charity. They already give/gave to Audubon and the Sierra Club.

OR: i.e., you're a respected local theatre company. They already give/gave to something similar in your arts-loving community.

Bottom line: your list is solid.

And your offer is everything it needs to be. (Training required.)

And the letter is everything it needs to be, too. (More training required.) The letter is warm. Stirring. Entertaining. Personal. Easy to read. Has a P.S. And obeys a dozen other well-tested rules of the direct mail craft.

So, how *will* you do? Perfect list, perfect offer, perfect letter?

If you get a 1 percent return, break out the champagne. Oh, heck, if you get a 0.5 percent response, have a stiff celebratory drink. How do you like *those* apples? One-half of one percent response? You sent out two hundred appeals. You got a single gift back, from a stranger. And YET—surprise!—you actually did *quite well*. You *met* industry standards.

How does it feel? Pretty good, right?

No?

Oh, those nasty assumptions

There's a bunch of nasty assumptions out there. Don't let them cloud your thinking:

- *We could get a 100 percent response rate.* (Giggle.)

- *The Shiny New Thing will save us.* (Delusional.) The SNT saves one, rarely two and surely not you.

  Crowdfunding? Two-thirds who try it don't make even a modest goal. Your very own Ice Bucket Challenge? Less chance than an asteroid strike on your windshield. Facebook fundraising? Works incredibly well for some charities (puppies and kittens are good). Requires training and testing and money.

  Is your charity willing to invest money to make money?

  I can tell you the answer in ninety-nine out of one hundred cases I've met: NO! Charities won't invest in anything . . .

whether it's the Shiny New Thing or the Shiny Tried and True Thing . . . like bequest marketing, which has an ROI of something like one hundred-to-one.

- *Anyone can be our donor.* (NRA members do not give to Brady gun control. Values must match.)

- *Any donor is a great donor.* (WRONG!) Yes, we *do* insist as one of the core values of "donor-centricity": *All donors are created equal.*

But, from a "money" point-of-view, they're not all equal. Most gave just once. Others quit pretty quickly. And a very few kept giving.

Look, I'll buy *any* new donor a beer (or whatever). It takes unusual willpower to escape inertia, which is comfortable and costs you nothing . . . and actually DO something to help. Most don't. So, bravo! Case in point: people *love* National Public Radio. Even people who don't *agree* politically, *they* love NPR, as polling reveals.

Yet how many of these "lovers" give to NPR's incessant but necessary fund drives? Six percent of frequent listeners? Seven percent maybe? I've never heard any higher percentage.

- *Once acquired, a new donor is likely to stay a long time.* "Ours for life." (See chapter 5.)

- *We need younger donors.* (See chapter 1.)

- *Grants and events are enough.* (Not if you want to grow. Foundations, businesses and government give relatively little. Events, by themselves, are not enough; they'll keep the lights on but that's about it. Individual households in America contribute about 80 percent of all charity every year; that's where your growth lies.)

The school-bus-yellow envelope stood out in a crowded mailbox. And the envelope teaser asked a question: "Are you a true believer?" It's the most important question you can ask. On an envelope, it's the first thing seen, seen within a second.

Direct mail professionals categorize questions as "involvement devices," a hunch now confirmed by neuroscience. The mere *presence* of a question mark makes literate human brains snap to attention. You can watch the reaction in MRIs. Question marks are like magic wands at Hogwarts: they make things happen.

One other thing made this direct mail appeal highly effective (in just a few weeks, it raised many tens of thousands in gifts). The envelope TELLS its recipients exactly what to do next, in inch-tall red letters: **OPEN THIS!**

All of us use mental shortcuts to make life's rapid-fire decision making faster and simpler and easier. Being told what to do next is a mental shortcut . . . and welcome.

This appeal for first-time donors did great. The list was airtight: only people who knew The Steel Yard personally were on it. Maybe they'd taken courses there. Or attended spectacular events there. Or had shopped in the Saturday farmer's market there.

CHAPTER 11

Know your SMIT

How often in a single appeal
can you ask for a gift?

[ ] Once is enough
[ ] Three or four times is OK
[ ] Sky's the limit

Thank you, Dr. Siegfried Vögele (1931–2014).

Professor Vögele uncovered how people *really* read direct mail.

Senders assume it's straightforward: the recipient opens the envelope, reads the contents, decides yes or no.

Not even close.

For instance, "Before your letter is read line by line, the recipient skims over the whole page in one cursory glance."

None of us knew that until Vögele observed the behavior in his Munich laboratory, as average people fumbled their way through commercial direct mail.

The professor also discovered that, during that initial cursory glance, certain things act as "eye magnets": bulleted lists, highlighted stuff, margin notes, art, photos, subheads and other briefer

le words on a line stand out and draw attention to
he reported. Single words like . . .

So, again: thank you, Dr. Vögele. An industry that relies heavily on direct mail for its financial health (as major-league fundraising does) owes you a lot. If there isn't yet a Vögele prize, there should be. It should be awarded each year to the research that overturns the biggest misconception.

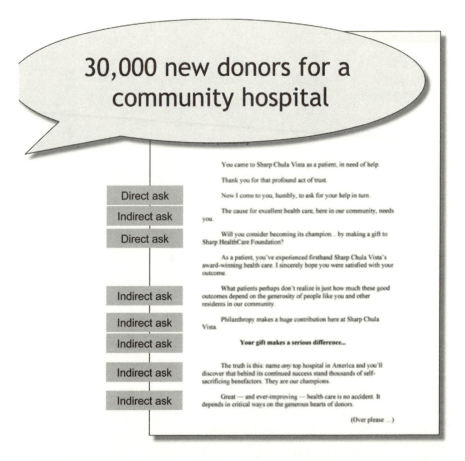

Over the years, this letter was used by a system of hospitals in San Diego to turn tens of thousands of discharged patients into first-time donors. I labeled all the direct ("please make a gift") and indirect ("gifts are essential") asks. As you see, the appeal's relentless. It knows its SMIT: "Ask for help from the people who know you best and care about you most: satisfied ex-patients."

Don't do this

Where did we all learn to be so reticent about asking for help?

Each year, I see scores of fundraising appeals written by newbies. Many share a deadly habit: waiting to the end of the letter to make "the ask."

Don't wait to ask. Ask early . . . within the first few sentences. Ask often . . . in the middle, repeatedly . . . and at the end, just before the signature. Then ask again in the P.S. *And* on the reply device. *And* on the giving page of your charity's website.

Ask. Ask. Ask.

Again. Again. Again.

Why? Return to Siegfried Vögele's research.

People do *not* read your appeals in a linear fashion. Their eyes (Vögele discovered) flit like butterflies, seeking things of interest.

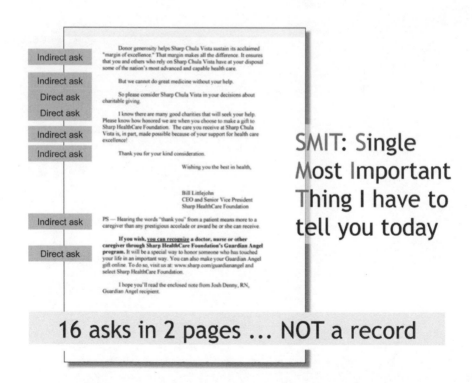

SMIT: Single Most Important Thing I have to tell you today

16 asks in 2 pages ... NOT a record

Meet the SMIT, an idea introduced by Pareto, Australia's biggest direct mail (and telephone) fundraising agency. SMIT is an acronym. It stands (incompletely) for "Single Most Important Thing I have to tell you today."

Don't be shy. Don't be confused. For many appeals, mailed or emailed, the SMIT is simply to ask for help.

CHAPTER 12

Event ROI (return on investment)

Are fundraising events important
to a charity's success?

[ ] Yes
[ ] No
[ ] Maybe

A fundraiser in Tasmania had this question: "Wondering if anyone has any thoughts or articles on ROI. Just got my annual business plan back with the comment that events are [expected] to achieve 300% ROI . . . after including wage costs. Help!!"

Is a 300 percent ROI for events reasonable or unreasonable?

I don't know. Guru Roger Craver calls ROI an "efficiency metric." You spend a dollar. Now how much will that dollar raise?

- Direct mail appeals sent to current donors can return $2 or $3 or even $4 for every $1 spent.
- The ROI for events and grants at smaller organizations can range from two-to-one to five-to-one, research found.
- I know print donor newsletters that return seven-to-one or higher ROI.

- I know Facebook fundraising that gets seven-to-one on a slow day and twenty-five-to-one when disaster strikes and you're riding serious news coverage.

- An effective major gifts officer can raise ten times her salary.

- Bequest marketing can pay off ten thousand-to-one.

Events? It's hard to tell.

I had a funny moment recently with a roomful of fundraisers in Windsor, Ontario. We were talking about ROI and such.

I asked them, "How many of you think events are worth doing?" Heads slammed into palms. Groans. Not a single hand went up.

So then I asked, "OK, none of you think they're worth doing. How many of you DO events?" Every hand went up.

Revealing . . . of something. Do we do events because they're worth doing or . . . do we do events because, compared to pretty much everything else in fundraising (except maybe writing grant applications), they're "easy enough that someone without much training can manage the task."

What makes an event "great"?

Events end up all over the place.

Some are cash cows. Some become community traditions, the date saved on countless calendars.

Springing to mind: the hedonistic Chocolate Affair that annually benefits Baltimore's Health Care for the Homeless.

Springing to mind: the wow-inspiring Jack-O-Lantern Spectacular at Roger Williams Park Zoo. In 2018, the Spectacular celebrated thirty years as must-see seasonal family entertainment in southeastern New England.

Yet many events are forgettable drudgeries for charity staff and volunteers: here today, gone tomorrow, producing little ROI. "Tell me again: why did we waste so much time on that? We had half as many people as last year!"

University researchers recently studied nonprofit events that had "**doubled or tripled** [emphasis added] either [the amount they raised or their number of participants] in a ten-year period or less."[15] Certain factors were common to these successes. Among the things that mattered most:

- **"Invest in the Team:"** There will be highs. And lows. "Managing these events can often be draining or even painful (i.e. deaths can occasionally occur in sporting and challenge events). A focus on wellbeing, therefore, helps build the resilience of the team to cope."

- **"Create Board Champions:** No matter how great the idea or how rosy the revenue forecast might be, an unsupportive management and board can still stifle many potentially outstanding events."

- **"Focus on Transformations, Not Experiences:** All of the events we examined were offering supporters a high-quality experience and we noted a general shift from planning the features of an event toward planning the experiences it would offer." Translation: it's not about educating or even entertaining donors. It's about *transforming* donors. Your basic goal: donors will FEEL differently about their connection to your charity AFTER the event.

- **"Focus Innovation on Fundamental Human Needs:"** Translation from academic-speak: successful events make donors feel VERY good about donating.

- **"A High Degree of Donor-Centricity:** . . . Many organisations pay only lip service to the notion of donor-centricity when in reality they care little about it." Does *your* event celebrate the donors who make your programs possible?

- **"Choose the Appropriate Mindset."** Translation: ask for gifts immediately, not later. Asking NOW raises more money. Asking LATER raises less.

Are you investing? And if not, *why* not?

Charity Navigator made it official in 2016: their 20 percent limit on overhead was inadequate.

Limiting. Stultifying. Dumb-ish. Counter-productive in a messed-up world that desperately needs stronger charities; not weak, scared organizations. Other self-anointed "watchdogs" soon followed suit.

Then on June 7, 2018, the *Chronicle of Philanthropy* published a scathing article by Amanda Pearce, CFRE, under the headline, "Nonprofit Is a Tax Status, NOT a Business Model."

Then, on September 20, 2018, *Science News* ran an article headlined, "Widely Used Nonprofit Efficiency Tool Doesn't Work." This article zeroed in on a troubling new discovery: "A recent study from North Carolina State University finds that the tool most often used to assess the efficiency of nonprofit organizations isn't just inaccurate—it can actually be negatively correlated with efficiency."

Dear nonprofit leadership: don't fall for this common scam.

If you want to *grow*, you *must* invest: you *must* take risks. "Except they're NOT risks," as one exasperated expert tweeted, "if they raise more money, bring in gobs more new donors, keep active donors longer and lead to bequests. Then they're wise investments."

Would your board do it?

Pretend you're a mid-sized nonprofit. You're not rich but you're not poor, either. The chief fundraiser asks the board to invest $100,000 over three years in a bequest-marketing program. The nonprofit has that kind of money, maybe in its contingency fund.

Would your board do it?

What if you had a *time machine* and could leap forward to PROVE to your board members that their approval of a one-time $100,000 investment would ... *within just three years* ... start a pipeline of charitable bequests flowing, bequests that would average (conservatively) a quarter-million dollars each ... and that within ten years, your organization would see dozens of new people joining your Legacy Society every year?

Would they invest the $100,000?

You tell me.

We don't have time machines handy. Really: no one can make that kind of guarantee. You *have* to take a risk. Even in Nonprofit Land, where unicorns roam: you invest money to make money.

By the way, that really happened.

A nonprofit board in Virginia invested $100,000 in a professionally competent bequest marketing effort ... and it paid off in many, many millions of new dollars coming in.

CHAPTER 13

A donate button is not enough

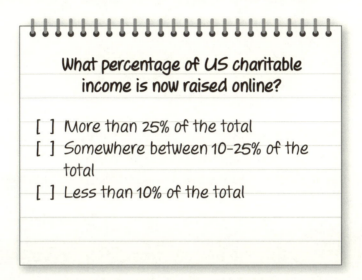

What percentage of US charitable
income is now raised online?

[ ] More than 25% of the total
[ ] Somewhere between 10-25% of the
total
[ ] Less than 10% of the total

The percentage of total fundraising that came from online giving reached another record high in 2017. About 7.6% of overall fundraising revenue, excluding grants, was raised online. . . . This is the continuation of a growth trend Blackbaud has measured over many years now.

Technology has changed everything.

- It's bred new kinds of habits and addictions. A 2017 study by global tech protection and support company Asurion reported in the New York Post that Americans check their smartphones every 12 minutes, 80 times a day.

- It's changed education. You can now earn graduate degrees online, from respected universities, not just mills.

- It's changed how we communicate. IM, Facebook, Twitter, Instagram, WhatsApp, Skype (to name just a few) have burrowed beneath the skin of daily life.

- It's changed how we pay bills and transfer money. (I love PayPal.)

- It's changed entertainment. (Smart TVs. Streaming.)

- It's changed how we date. (I hear; married thirty-plus years)

And the heavy presence of technology in our lives *has* DEFINITELY changed how people donate to charity. Just not as fast as you might worry. You haven't missed the boat. The boat's still being built.

Look, print's been around since 1440-ish. Movable type led to mass literacy. Which led to mass advertising. Which led to newspapers, magazines, radio, television and now this, the technology invasion. Online giving's been around since what . . . at its earliest, 1995?

On the other hand, behaviors are changing. What raked in loads of donations "in the day" doesn't work quite the same anymore, not with average Americans now spending twenty-four hours a week online and 82 percent of us accessing the internet and our email from smartphones.

Take direct mail, for instance. Online giving didn't *replace* direct mail giving. Online *augmented* direct mail. The physical letter arrives, reminding me, "Oh, yeah. I like that charity. It's probably time to give." Which I do . . . *not* by writing a check but by going online . . . where I'm now accustomed to shop (I made my first online purchase in 1995).

It's called "channel shifting." I *used to* complete my gift with a check. Now I've shifted to online completion. In both cases, though, be aware: direct mail prompted the gift.

From: Michael Grace <friends@mos.org>
Date: November 27, 2018 at 10:04:40 AM EST
To: marci@boardontrack.com
Subject: Boston's biggest snow yet?
Reply-To: friends@mos.org

Get out your shovel!   View in browser

 Museum of Science.   #GI♥INGTUESDAY

Dear Friend,

February 17–18, President's Day, 2003: 27.6 inches of snow
falls on Boston in 24 hours, making it the biggest single day of
snow in Boston since modern recordkeeping began in 1892.

Until now.

**Today, November 27, 2018—Giving Tuesday—we're asking
for your help to bury our building up to the point of its**

I stopped counting when the one hundredth #GivingTuesday appeal hit my email in-box. This one from the Museum of Science in Boston stood out, though. It didn't mention #GivingTuesday in the subject line, for one thing. Instead, it mentioned something that I, as a New Englander, am always alert to: heavy snowfalls. Remember: the purpose of a subject line is to get your email opened . . . nothing else.

#GivingTuesday: Easy money, right?

Debuted in 2012 as a better-worlders' counterweight to the consumer feeding frenzies of Black Friday and Cyber Monday, #GivingTuesday occupies the first Tuesday after the annual US Thanksgiving holiday. The 92nd Street Y and the United Nations Foundation in New York City launched the idea.

And it *took:* big time.

Food for the Poor keeps it simple. They show you the problem (starving children, no place to sleep). They invite you to become some child's solution, at a very affordable price. And they overtly connect with your pre-existing Christian values.

Online donations for #GivingTuesday rose 52 percent in 2015, the fourth year of the event, with 17 percent of those gifts being made on a mobile device such as an iPad or iPhone. Globally, #GivingTuesday reaped $117 million that year.

And it just gets bigger every year: 2016 = $168 million, 44 percent growth year over year; 2017 = $274 million, 63 percent growth year over year, with an average gift in 2017 of $111.

Easy money?

In 2018, a terrific local literacy charity I know put some serious effort into promoting #Giving Tuesday to its base . . . and raised in total $75.

Let's get down in the mud: there IS *no* easy fundraising. You want #GivingTuesday to work flares-a-blazin' for your charity? Make it a priority. Beat that horse to death, from a promotional point of view, starting in August/September. Otherwise? Expect to be underwhelmed.

Nor is a donate button enough to increase giving online. The donate button on websites and in emails is now the world's most common element in online fundraising. Which means it's become incredibly trite and dismissible.

If you're not collecting many gifts online, it's high time you learned what you *don't* know. Because *some* nonprofits DO now harvest almost ALL their charity online; online fundraising is do-able.

CHAPTER 14

Wrong

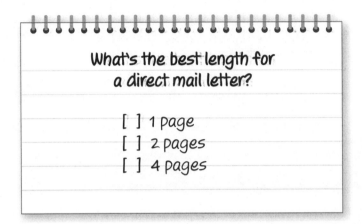

What's the best length for
a direct mail letter?

[ ] 1 page
[ ] 2 pages
[ ] 4 pages

This is what worries me.

It's 2018, in Maryland. There are about 150 nonprofit executives and fundraisers in the audience. And one asks, fully confident, "Since we know a one-page letter is the best length, doesn't that limit how big the type font can be?"

WHAT? We *don't* "know" that . . . on the contrary.

Look, it's not the page count that matters. It's the quality of the writing.

A four-page letter, written by someone with training, will almost always outperform a one-page letter. A lousy four-page letter will flop.

Among top direct mail professionals worldwide, there is zero debate: they expect to get their strongest results writing longer letters . . . and they test that assumption a lot.

- And we need you as a new Friend.

∼ What's your particular passion? ∼

Do you crave a walk in the great outdoors?

You can now enjoy 72 miles of developed country and urban trails along the river and its environs ... thanks in part to the persistence of FMR initiatives over the years.

And, you know, we're far from done. There's more to do. But we need more Friends like you to take it all on!

One of FMR's chief goals is to make the river accessible to more people. Right now, for instance, we're working with North Minneapolis communities, some of the city's least privileged, to access and enjoy the river that was always there ... but poisoned and unreachable behind industries that had turned its waters into a dead zone.

Are you a natural born bird-watcher?

Then you probably already know this: the Mississippi is one of the planet's busiest flyways.

I quote the experts: "It's a flyway that provides birds with direction, resting places and food. Songbirds that winter in Central and South America and 60% of North America's ducks, geese, swans and wading birds rely on the Mississippi River during their epic seasonal migrations."

∼ You will be proud. ∼

Show the world you've signed on.

Prominently post the "Friend of the Mississippi River" window cling I've enclosed. (Change your mind? No worries, no glue! Window clings stick by static. And they peel right off.)

4

Page 4 of a successful six-page acquisition letter. This particular letter increased membership in an environmental group 20 percent, with a single mailing. Analyze this page: there's a lot to be learned.

"Long letters pretty much always do better [in those tests]," Jeff Brooks told me. "And that's true for acquisition as well as donor cultivation."

And why wouldn't they? Professionally written letters work hard to entertain you, to grab you, to keep you on the edge of your seat, to draw you in and onward. Masterful letters are fast, built for skimming. They're warm and flattering. They tell a vivid story of urgent need . . . and treat you, the donor, as a hero.

Most charities are stuck with letters written by the un- or slightly trained. Let's be clear: with those letters, shorter is better. State your case, make your ask, be grateful, be polite, be brief and be gone.

To succeed consistently with direct mail, you must get training. At a minimum, read the frequently updated classic, Mal Warwick's *How to Write Successful Fundraising Appeals*. The latest edition (2013) covers both postal and emailed appeals. And for good measure, and an even deeper understanding of the writer's thought process, get a copy of Jeff Brooks's *The Fundraiser's Guide to Irresistible Communications* or his latest, *How to Turn Your Words into Money*.

CHAPTER 15

Grade level and speed reading

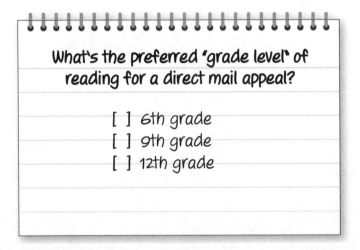

What's the preferred "grade level" of
reading for a direct mail appeal?

[ ] 6th grade
[ ] 9th grade
[ ] 12th grade

You're not sure, right? Well, what if I told you that this *particular* direct mail appeal hoped to raise donations from alumni of a prestigious university?

In that case, you might assume "twelfth grade." The thinking: write at the same grade level as a person's educational attainment.

Otherwise you commit the insult of "writing down."

Not exactly

"Grade level," as measured by the standard Flesch-Kincaid readability scoring system, has nothing to do with your intelligence or how far you went in school.

The system scores just one thing:

How quickly *my* brain can move through *your* prose.

Below, on the left, are the readability scores for a successful direct mail letter. On the right are the readability scores for a university-written case for support. The one on the left will be a brisk read for everyone. The one on the right will be a slog for everyone, including the PhDs.

You decide.

Your writing can bring me clarity and quick understanding. Or your writing can bring me labor. Which do you think is more "reader convenient" . . . or appreciated?

Readability Statistics	
Counts	
Words	306
Characters	1586
Paragraphs	28
Sentences	31
Averages	
Sentences per Paragraph	1.6
Words per Sentence	8.4
Characters per Word	4.9
Readability	
Passive Sentences	0%
Flesch Reading Ease	69.6
Flesch–Kincaid Grade Level	5.6

Readability Statistics	
Counts	
Words	1828
Characters	10439
Paragraphs	32
Sentences	78
Averages	
Sentences per Paragraph	4.1
Words per Sentence	21.8
Characters per Word	5.6
Readability	
Passive Sentences	10%
Flesch Reading Ease	23.9
Flesch–Kincaid Grade Level	12.0

Writing at a lower grade level is not about talking *down*. It's about talking *clearly*.

You can write about astrophysics at the eighth-grade level. (And if you're writing for a general audience, you should.)

In fact, grade level and reading ease scores have little to do with vocabulary. A computer decides your score, after all. And that computer isn't "reading." It's counting. It's calculating ratios of long to short. If most of your sentences are simply constructed, if you keep multisyllabic words to a minimum, you'll do fine.

The preceding paragraph scores at the sixth-grade level, by the way. Did it seem like I was talking down to you?

Pennsylvania and many other states now require that insurance policies score no higher than the ninth-grade level on

Flesch-Kincaid. Novels written for airport bookstores score at the fourth-grade level. And the *Wall Street Journal* hovers around the ninth-grade level, reporting on everything under the sun.

The back story

Where did Flesch-Kincaid scoring originate? With the US Navy.

You must have a high school diploma to enlist in the navy. Yet you might end up operating and fixing some of the world's most sophisticated technology (fighter jets, nuclear power plants, that stuff). The problem was the technical manuals. Engineers wrote them. But non-engineers used them.

The US Navy commissioned J. Peter Kincaid, a psychologist and university professor, to come up with a way to test the prose: is it easy enough for someone with only a high school diploma to understand?

Kincaid verified and applied the methods and insights of Dr. Rudolf Flesch (1911–1986).

Flesch, a Viennese lawyer who fled the Nazis and resettled in New York, published many books on the subject of clear, effective communication. *Time* magazine dubbed him the "Mr. Fix-It of writing." He was also known as "the man who taught Associated Press how to write." I have his 1949 book, *The Art of Readable Writing*, a gift from Steve Herlich. But Flesch's most famous book became *Why Johnny Can't Read: And What You Can Do about It.* That book inspired Dr. Seuss to write *The Cat in the Hat.*

Flesch-Kincaid scoring became the Department of Defense's military standard for all technical manuals.

The preceding two paragraphs score at the eighth-grade level. Did it seem like I was talking down to you?

Final word goes to the late, great George Smith (1940–2012), writer for Oxfam, Amnesty, Greenpeace, UNICEF, WWF and many more. He said, "All fundraising copy should sound like someone talking."

The grade level of conversation is low.

CHAPTER 16

"Looks unprofessional"

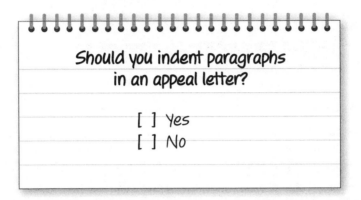

Should you indent paragraphs
in an appeal letter?

[ ] Yes
[ ] No

Should you indent? This rudimentary formatting question comes up surprisingly often.

In part it arises, I think, because nonprofit organizations aren't quite sure: Is an appeal a *personal* letter or a *business* letter?

Let's end that confusion.

An appeal for a gift from an individual should mimic as much as possible the kind of letter you'd send a friend.

The more personal (or, to say it another way, the *less* corporate) it is, the more likely it is to raise money.

Business-writing consultant Lynn Gaertner-Johnston calls the un-indented, "full-block style" of letter "modern and sleek." She deems indented letters "fussy and dated looking." And don't we want our organization to seem at least modern, if not sleek?

Not really.

As direct mail master Jeff Brooks notes with approval: "Ugly works. Tacky works. Corny, embarrassing, and messy all work. In print, or in digital."

Pattern recognition (speed reading 101)

But, look, this is the wrong discussion. We *should* be talking about reader convenience and the role of pattern recognition in reducing the labor of reading.

- Your brain is in training every time you enjoy a novel. The paragraphs of that novel will be indented.

- Your brain is in training every time you pick up a newspaper. The paragraphs of that newspaper will be indented.

- Your brain is in training every time you dig into a magazine article. The paragraphs of that article will be indented.

I.e., most of the time you're reading *indented* prose.

WOW! Do you know how AMAZING you are??

So amazing that I think about you every day.
And not in a weird way.

I'm an admirer, not a stalker. Promise.

And although I may not know you personally,
I do know a few things about you:

You care. A lot.

You make a difference. *Every day.*

You are loved. That's right. *Loved.*

Without you, the lives of homeless, abandoned, and neglected animals in our community
would look very different. And not in a good way. Because without you, the work we do to
help those who have no one else doesn't happen. Can't happen. Won't happen.

So as you go about your day today, and every day, I hope you feel joy in your heart. Joy in
knowing you matter. That your compassion is saving lives. That you inspire me and our team
every day to keep fighting the good fight.

And I hope you enjoy the enclosed newsletter. It is filled with the miracles you make happen
with your generosity. Thank you for being a part of our LIFE SAVING family!

Your biggest fan,

Julie

P.S.   I'd love to hear what you think about the revamped newsletter! You can find me at
JEdwards@HSNEGA.org or 770-532-6617 (when I'm not cuddling puppies, of course!) :)

Corny is something of a specialty at Toronto's Agents of Good, a creative agency
serving charities. Humbert "the custodian of donor care" successfully introduced
a local community to its new "all digital" hospital." And then there's Julie Edwards,
executive director. She admits, "I'm loud!" And being corny suits her to a T, as this
cover letter for her donor newsletter shows. Of course, being corny has a serious
goal: to make more money for your mission.

Here's the issue: our brains depend on various visual cues to speed things along. That's called "pattern recognition." And chief among these visual cues? The common indent.

Remove indents, and you get the opposite effect: slower comprehension, not faster. Subconsciously, the brain labors a little more: never a good thing when you're asking me for my hard-earned money.

Typographic expert Ilene Strizver states, "The purpose of an indent is to create a visual separation between paragraphs." She then adds, "When you have room to spare and want a cleaner, more open look, separate the paragraphs with an extra line space instead of an indent."

Irene's right.

But I'm a belt-and-suspenders kind of appeal writer: I use both indents *and* extra line spaces between paragraphs! And so do all the other high-performance direct mail writers and creative houses I know around the world . . . at least, most of the time.

". . . with as much anticipation as possible"

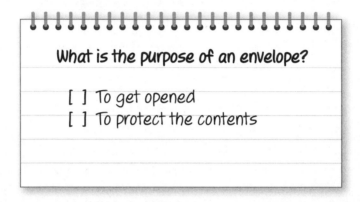

What is the purpose of an envelope?

[ ] To get opened
[ ] To protect the contents

If you're paying a bill with a check, or mailing your lover a tender letter, the envelope's purpose is defense: protect the contents.

But then there's today's world of direct mail appeals.

That world is different.

"Most Americans have never heard of Jerry Huntsinger," the *New York Times* wrote, "but they have probably heard from him. Mr. Huntsinger, 64, is a direct-mail fund-raiser, one of the best in the business."

Here is Jerry's dictum, as I first learned it: "The envelope: the purpose is to get it ripped open with as much anticipation as possible. Nothing else."

The average mailbox is a rough, dismissive neighborhood. "If one recipient in 50 opens the envelope," *New York Times* reported, "Mr. Huntsinger calls his campaign a success."

Renewal appeals are different

The *New York Times* article and Jerry Huntsinger were talking primarily about envelopes used for "acquisition" appeals. Such appeals hope to attract (i.e., "acquire") first-time donors. New donors. Fresh faces.

"Renewal" appeals are different. They're respectful and thankful and they ask those who have given before (i.e., your supporter family, your members, your so-called "base") to please give again.

Successful renewal envelopes and successful acquisition envelopes can look as different as night and day.

Here's what I learned in Oslo in 2018.

Norges Blindeforbund (the Norwegian Association of the Blind, founded in 1900; the country's oldest advocacy group for the disabled), relies heavily on fundraising direct mail.

What works best in acquisition are colorful envelopes bearing big teaser messages. A perennial "best-selling" offer is the group's annual calendar featuring portraits of guide dogs.

What works best in renewal appeals, though, are plain envelopes bearing nothing but the organization's logo and address.

Why plain envelopes sometimes work better . . . even for donor acquisition

Jeff Brooks is one of the world's most experienced direct mail fundraisers. He freely shares what he's learned in his Future Fundraising Now blog. In the following post, he offers a keen insight:

> Teaser-free envelopes out-perform those with teasers more often than not. I'm not the first to have noted this. Probably anyone who's done a lot of direct mail testing knows this.

> But the reason many people give for the success of teaser-free envelopes is this: *A teaser doesn't work because it makes a piece of mail look junky.*

Now we can't know for sure why things work and don't work. But I'm pretty sure that particular reason is **dead wrong**.

Here's what makes me think so: I have seldom seen a nicer, more classy, more professional piece of direct mail out-perform a more junky piece. Time after time, junk beats class. Did I say "beats"? I should say *junk kicks class's butt*. Hands down, nearly every time.

Seriously, if you want to improve your results, make your mail uglier. That's how consistent that pattern is.

So I'm confident that a teaser-less envelope usually wins for some other reason than it looks less junky. My own explanation is that *most teasers are lame*. The typical teaser is basically like this:

> WARNING! There is an appeal for money inside. It's a lot like all the other appeals for money you get. If you read it, you'll be uncomfortable until you either forget or write a check. Take your pick. Oh yeah: there are some free address labels inside too.

Nobody tries to write teasers like that. But that's how most of them come out.

Saying nothing at all is better than saying something lame.

44 School Street, Suite 400
Boston, Massachusetts 02108

You can turn these
into a high school
diploma

44 School Street, Suite 400
Boston, Massachusetts 02108

Top: An envelope seeking new donors, with a teaser (image and words). **Bottom:** the same envelope without that teaser. No one can predict which will work better. You just have to test. Copy: Tina Cincotti, Funding Change Consulting. Design: Wendy Brovold.

CHAPTER 18

Research said

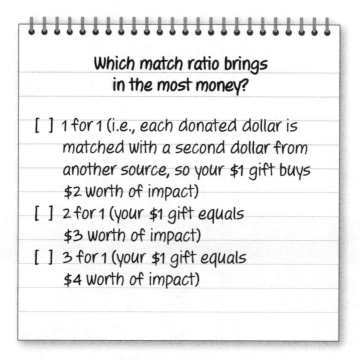

Which match ratio brings
in the most money?

[ ] 1 for 1 (i.e., each donated dollar is
matched with a second dollar from
another source, so your $1 gift buys
$2 worth of impact)

[ ] 2 for 1 (your $1 gift equals
$3 worth of impact)

[ ] 3 for 1 (your $1 gift equals
$4 worth of impact)

Even the researchers were surprised.
Economists John List (University of Chicago) and Dean Karlan (Yale University) ran the same experiment twice, to make sure. Both times, a three-for-one match did no better than a one-for-one match.

The *presence* of a matching-gift offer was the stimulus, not the size of the *ratio*.

"The offer to match increased both the revenue per solicitation and the probability that an individual donates," they reported.

"Simply announcing the availability of the match increased revenue per solicitation by 19%. However, larger match [ratios] had no additional impact on propensity to donate or donation amount."

They concluded: offering a three-to-one match instead of a one-to-one match won't hurt response. It just won't *improve* response.

What *can* hurt response is how you talk about the offer.

In later research, List and Karlan found "that when the example matching amount is $25 instead of $1 (i.e., 'For example, if you give $75, the matching donor will give $25' versus 'For example, if you give $3, the matching donor will give $1'), then the ratio of the match *does* matter, in particular for those who have not given before. In this case, the larger example amount actually causes *harm*."

Go figure.

Yes, I want my donation to make **five times** the difference to cancer patients

Step 1: My gift

☐ \<Ask 1\>   ☐ \<Ask 2\>   ☐ \<Ask 3\>   ☐ My choice $ _____

Step 2: I would like to make my gift by:

☐ Cheque/money order made payable to Eastern Health Foundation

☐ VISA   ☐ Mastercard   ☐ AMEX   ☐ Diners

Card no.: __ __ __ __ / __ __ __ __ / __ __ __ __ / __ __ __ __

Expiry: __ __ / __ __

Name on card: _____

Signature: _____

If you give before 17 Dec your gift will be matched

✖5

by a private donor.

Common sense leads us to assume that a five-to-one match will attract more donations than a one-to-one match. The List/Karlan research found otherwise. But then there are Jeff Brooks' experiences. Guidelines, not rules.

On the other hand

It's reassuring to think that the same principles will work the same way for everyone everywhere every time. And they do . . . until they don't.

The List/Karlan research was rigorous and replicated. But research has it limits. We're not talking physics and immutable laws, after all. We're talking fundraising. And human behavior varies.

Jeff Brooks has at this point in his long career been involved in hundreds of direct mail campaigns offering matches. "My testing," he tweeted late in 2018, "found the bigger the match, the better. 3x worked better than 2x, meaningfully but not dramatically. Tested as high as 2,150x (that's not a typo!) and it all worked, bigger numbers outpulling smaller."

So, again: go figure.

As the cunning Captain Barbossa cautioned his captive, Elizabeth Swann, "[The Pirate's] code is more what you'd call 'guidelines' than actual rules."

There are few hard-and-fast, black-and-white "rules" in donor communications. We have, instead, guidelines and probabilities and likelihoods and *educated* opinions (*uneducated* opinions should go out with the trash) . . . with a sprinkling of fresh research and psychological insights added each year to keep us on our toes.

CHAPTER 19

More is more, up to a point

How often can you ask in a year
without driving off donors?

[ ] Once a year
[ ] Three times a year
[ ] A dozen times a year
[ ] Twenty-one times year

Stick with me; this gets tricky.

We were at the first Nonprofit Storytelling Conference in Seattle. Mid-November 2014. The hall held a rare concentration of top experts. Next to me at the table sat Jeff Brooks, at the time a senior copywriter at one of America's best direct mail firms.

A fundraiser in the audience asked a seemingly simple question: "How often can you ask in a year without losing donors?"

The answer?

I glanced at Jeff. He flashed the number twenty with his fingers. *Really?*

Then another fundraiser took the floor to describe a test he'd done, to see what the limit was. His charity mailed twenty-one solicitations in a year before gifts tapered off. These were postal mail, too; not email.

Are twenty-one solicitations really all that intrusive? It comes down to less than two solicitations per month. During the last US presidential campaign, more than two emailed solicitations *per day* hit my in-box from the candidate I favored.

Veteran Steven Screen, co-founder of Better Fundraising, shared this insight at the 2018 Nonprofit Storytelling Conference: "In 20 years, I've only come across one organization that was asking for donations too often. The sweet spot is thirty-six times a year."

But seriously

Over-solicitation is probably NOT your charity's problem.

Most charities are nowhere close to twenty-one solicitations a year. Which means you might be leaving some serious money on the table. It could be yours if you just asked a few more times.

In answer to the question "How many times a year should I mail my donors?" Canadian expert Alan Sharpe advises, "Mail at least eight times a year. Mail at least four appeal letters and mail at least four newsletters (or donor cultivation, donor information type pieces)."

It's funny, though

In focus groups, donors complain long and loud about being over-solicited by their favorite charities.

The catch? If you watch their behavior, you will see that they actually don't stop giving as a result.

Fabienne, my French cousin-in-law, is a perfect example. She's a retired teacher; happily married with one beloved adult son. And she's got a big heart. She gives to about two dozen charities a year, prompted by direct mail. She's given to some for decades.

And the ONLY thing she doesn't like about them and will sharply criticize is over-solicitation. "I give every year," she steams. "Why do they send me appeals all the time?" She sees it as wasteful. Her opinion, in sum: "Spend that money on the mission, not extra mailings!" Yet . . . despite this "appeal harassment" and a presumption of donor fatigue . . . Fabienne continues to give to the same charities year after year.

In the October 3, 2013, issue of The Agitator, Roger Craver reported, "Bottom line: Across a range of studies on donors to 250+ nonprofits in the US and the UK conducted by our colleagues at DonorVoice over the past four years, there is absolutely no evidence that frequency of solicitation negatively impacts retention and lifetime value. Period."

In fact, maybe just the opposite?

In November 2014, the CEO of Grizzard, Chip Grizzard, reported on some surprising test results. In the test, donors of $500 or more were allowed to limit the number of appeals they'd receive in the coming year. If they didn't specify otherwise, they'd receive twelve appeals. "Of the 500 in the group," Chip wrote, "186 [37%] wrote back and designated the specific mailings they wanted during the next 12-month mailing cycle. Interestingly, the most mailings anyone selected was three."

The end-of-year results surprised everyone. "The donors who received all 12 mailings gave 35% more than the ones [who'd limited their appeals]." The conclusion drawn? Unless a major donor asks you to limit mailings, stick with your normal mailing calendar. "You never know when something will strike a donor's fancy. Each appeal is different."

Jeff Brooks commented, "There's an important lesson here: **Less mail, less giving.** That's true in nearly every situation. Including major donors. Never assume donors will give more or retain longer if they get less contact. It almost never works that way."

And . . . don't over-react to complaints about over-solicitation, either. They're probably false alarms. And certainly don't listen to the timid amongst us who fret, "We'll drive off our donors if we ask too often." While it sounds reasonable, even polite and considerate, the science says it's dead wrong. The correct view is, "We'll leave a lot of money on the table if we don't ask often enough."

One last thing: about terminology.

Since I've tripped over this peculiar misunderstanding more than once, let's be clear: when we talk about an "annual fund," the word "annual" has nothing to do with asking just once a year. Rather, it has to do with what you're raising money for: your charity's annual operating expenses.

No need to speak French to understand "extrême urgence" or "enfants soldats." You're looking at a tiny fraction of the direct mail my cousin-in-law, Fabienne, receives each year in France. (She saves it for me.) Yes, she still gives to her favorite causes. But she believes that these same charities waste money on too-frequent mailers. Your challenge? Overturning that persistent and negative perception.

CHAPTER 20

Easy fixes

If you "raise awareness" in your
community, you'll raise more money.

[ ] Yes
[ ] No
[ ] Maybe

A board member grouses, "I told my friend I'd joined this board and he asked, 'What do they do?' He'd never heard of us! How am I supposed to help raise money if no one's ever heard of us?"

The chair sighs: "I really wish we had more visibility." The executive director gets a determined look: "We need to raise awareness!"

It's obvious, right?

If only your charity could get some coverage in the local news media, donors, like stampeding longhorns, would bust down your doors.

Sober up.

Fundraising is a marketing discipline. Success depends on your training, planning, commitment and investment.

And fundraising is never easy. Worshipping *pretend* tactics like "increased visibility"—rather than grappling with the greasy mechanics of fundraising and its vast body of knowledge—is irresponsible from a fiduciary standpoint.

Let's agree that your nonprofit's work is incredible, innovative, righteous and worthy of support from your entire community.

And then (hallelujah!) the local newspaper . . . or a local online news service . . . or even some big-cheese talk-radio personality in your area notices you for one news cycle.

What happens next?

Maybe two people contact you.

If the talk-show person included a strong call to action, maybe ten people contact you. Maybe *nobody* contacts you. In fact, it's likely that nobody contacts you. Nor will you go viral over social media, because just one in a million things do. Those odds are NOT in your favor.

Three top experts agree

Up first: Jeff Brooks, from his (essential and free) blog, Future Fundraising Now:

> Some "marketing experts" would have you believe fundraising is a two-step process: First you must make prospective donors "aware" of your organization, then you can ask them to give.

> Two-step fundraising is a colossal waste of money. You basically double your cost and get nothing in return. The truth is, if you have limited resources, there's almost no way you can justify spending them on awareness campaigns. For the awareness campaign to be worthwhile, it would have to improve fundraising by 67%. If you've been in fundraising for more than a couple of years, you know how unlikely that is. The reality is that most awareness campaigns make *no measurable difference* for fundraising campaigns.

Up second: Tobin Aldrich, who, among other achievements, led World Wildlife Fund UK to new fundraising heights. He wrote in his blog:

> One of those counter-intuitive things about fundraising is that people don't actually have to have heard about your charity before [they'll] respond to a fundraising ask. I've lost count of the times I've been told by smart, senior people with a marketing background in some famous company that the first thing <insert name of non-profit here> must do is get our name out or raise awareness of the cause. Only then should we start asking for money. So let's start with a big awareness raising campaign (hey, maybe we could get an ad agency to do it for free!)
>
> Sorry but that's bollocks basically. The first thing any non-profit should do is fundraise. When you fundraise you tell people about your cause, you make them care about it and they give you money as a result. And do you know what, you raise money and awareness too. It's amazing, isn't it?

Up last: Ireland's Ask Direct founder, Damian O'Broin. He ran a real-world test on "awareness."
Results?

- If your charity spent £500,000 on competent direct mail fund-raising, you brought in four thousand gifts.

- If your charity put £200,000 into awareness with the other £300,000 put into direct mail fundraising, you brought in three thousand gifts: 25 percent fewer. Why would anyone do that?

Generally (see exception below), "raising awareness" is a passive, wait-and-see, hope-and-pray approach. Whereas successful fundraising is intense and proactive: "Let's get to work, people! We have to get out there and ask!"

In fundraising, set SMART goals.

That acronym stands for Specific, Measurable, Agreed Upon, Realistic, Time-based. SMART goals sound like this: "The goal of our fourth-quarter direct mail appeal will be to increase membership in our organization by 10 percent."

DUMB (Daft, Unrealistic, Misunderstood, Backwards) goals sound like this: "We need to raise community awareness. Money will follow."

There are exceptions . . . *if* you're good at PR

In 2017, Mike McKenna, community engagement coordinator at Wood River Land Trust in Idaho, wrote me to say, "I think you are seriously missing the boat with this advice—and we've got the checks to prove it!"

Mike was reporting on a media campaign he ran that raised "nearly a million dollars in less than a month."

Mike is a fifteen-year veteran journalist and editor. He knows angles. He knows stories. He knows what exactly sells to news outlets. Here's a bit of what Mike did:

> By creating strong relationships with local and regional media members in particular—and by trying to customize what we create for them so that it will interest their followers/fanbases—we've been able to increase awareness and then directly our financial support.

Mike credits press releases "sent to the right sources" for raising nearly a million dollars in less than a month. "All with no hard costs for advertising, just a little staff time to write and disseminate the information, which we also shared via social media and direct emails to our current donors—who did not supply as much money as the random people who walked in off the streets to donate."

It didn't stop there either: "We also put on a free public event/concert this year that not only provided thousands in random donations [and] gained us contact information from hundreds of potential donors, all while getting tons of touches and helping brand ourselves to thousands who attended or saw the ample media coverage."

A smart, integrated, relentless public relations campaign can work . . . if you've got a pro like Mike McKenna helping you get the word out and coordinating the effort.

Mostly, though, local press coverage will not solve your fundraising problems. Don't be fooled: it's *not* a quick fix.

CHAPTER 21

Generosity in America

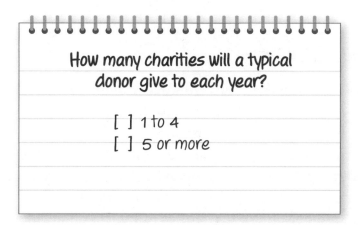

How many charities will a typical
donor give to each year?

[ ] 1 to 4
[ ] 5 or more

Generosity in America is a well-established social norm. In 2015, the majority of US households (67 percent) gave to charity, donating about 4 percent of their household income. Households that itemized their taxes gave away on average around $5,500, the Motley Fool reported.

Where does that charity go? Although religion customarily consumes the biggest slice of the US philanthropic pie (31 percent of all US giving in 2017; next largest: education with 14 percent), seldom does a household give to just one cause.

Research amongst Canadian donors found that almost half gave to between six and ten charities a year. More than a third of Canadian donors reported giving to more than twenty charities in a year.

What does that tell us about American giving habits?

"Americans are about twice as generous in their private giving as our kissing cousins the Canadians," the Philanthropy Roundtable estimated in 2016, using data from several sources, "and 3–15 times as charitable as the residents of other developed nations. Americans also volunteer more than almost any other wealthy people."

Love is hard (and easy)

Donors aren't monogamous. You share "your" donors with other causes. As UK expert Mark Phillips observed: "They are not *your* donors; you are one of *their* charities."

And every year, more charities come knocking, begging for support. My household supports at least two dozen charities right now. I can't even list them all for you, off the top of my head.

The number of public charities in the US almost doubled in the past fifteen years.

In fact, according to a 2018 *Fast Company* article, the US non-profit sector is now the nation's third largest employer, after retail and manufacturing. Nor is the US exceptional in that regard: explosive growth in the charity sector is a worldwide phenomenon.

So, how can your charity compete effectively in this hyper-crowded marketplace? The answer is surprisingly simple; and affordable; *and* within easy reach, when you put your mind to it.

Just be uncommonly good at the two things that *other* charities are generally poor at: thanking and reporting.

Great thanks are rare.

Great reporting—telling your donors exactly what their generous gifts accomplished in a hurting world—is almost nonexistent.

Do both well? You'll soon stand out from the crowd.

CHAPTER 22

Judging new donors

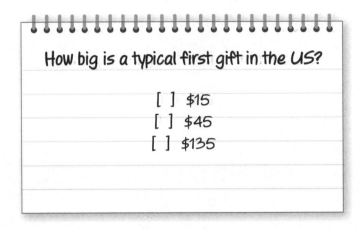

How big is a typical first gift in the US?

[ ] $15
[ ] $45
[ ] $135

B loomerang sits atop a mountain of data. Founded in 2012, Bloomerang is donor-management software tailored for nonprofits with annual budgets of $10 million or less. With its emphasis on easy use, the software now boasts thousands of satisfied clients. Most are local US and Canadian charities, representing millions of donors in total.

So, in November 2018, I asked Bloomerang the same question, "What's a typical first gift?" In a week, they delivered an answer: among Bloomerang clients, the median first gift from a new supporter is $45.

Small potatoes? No: *typical* potatoes.

Harvard and Jane

There's only so much a first gift tells us.

A first gift shows that the person may have some interest in your mission. But it shows you nothing about the person's true "giving capacity" or his ultimate lifetime value to your cause.

"When Harvard did a study after their last campaign," as Jerry Panas pointed out in 2017, "of their 254 million-dollar donors, 2 out of 3 started with first-time gifts of $100 or less."

The lesson? *Never* judge a donor by the size of her first gift.

They are called "first-date" gifts for a reason. The real question is: will your charity be beguiling enough to win a second date, so that maybe a romance will blossom?

A lot depends on you.

Some charities think it makes sense not to waste time on donors who make modest gifts. "We simply cannot thank anyone who gives us less than $25. We just don't have the time."

I say: treat every donor well . . . because you never know.

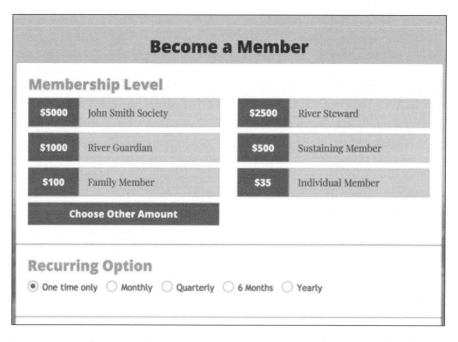

Do you expect first-time donors to march in, banners waving, shouting, "I'm rich . . . and I love you!" This kind of giving string on your sign-up page suggests you do. It also suggests that small-amount donors aren't all that welcome.

There's another phenomenon common in fundraising: the middle-class donor who gives loyally but little . . . who then leaves you big bucks in her will.

Case in point: Jane H. Kesson. Jane earned a master's in music composition from the University of Pennsylvania and became a K-12 music teacher. She lived with her parents and remained in her childhood home after they died. She never married.

"Music was her life," said a friend. And she adored the Philadelphia Orchestra, a twenty-five-minute drive from her home, "from the time she was 12." She volunteered there. She was a season subscriber. And she gave: not a lot, but every year.

One other thing about Jane: her dad taught her to save and invest. So throughout her long life she put money away. When she died in 2017 at age ninety, Jane Kesson, of average means to all appearances, left her beloved (and "flabbergasted") Philadelphia Orchestra $4.7 million.

Happens all the time.

CHAPTER 23

When inertia works *for* you

M onthly giving is better in so many ways.

- **It's easier for all concerned.** "Preauthorized monthly giving programs make donating automatic. This automation makes the process easy for the donor and the nonprofit."

- **Monthly donors tend to give more.** "According to the eNonprofits Benchmarks Study, monthly donors give an average of $228 per year while one-time donors only give an average of $60 per year. Several studies show that donors give more than double if they can separate the donation into smaller, preauthorized payments."

- **Donor retention rates are higher.** "The Nonprofit Times reports that the annual retention rate for monthly donors is 70% compared to 41–50% for donors who make one-time gifts."

- **Lifetime Value (LTV) is higher.** In 2015, researcher Professor Adrian Sargeant released a study revealing that the LTV of a monthly donor is six to eight times higher than the LTV of an annual donor.

- **Lower administrative costs** than direct mail.

- **Predictable income.** When a lot of your donors are monthly donors, income is easier to project.

- **You're communicating monthly, rather than occasionally.** Frequent touches help bond donors to your cause . . . even if it's nothing more than a credit card statement delivering the reminder.

- Monthly giving is **the route to younger donors**. They like it. They feel they can afford it.

- **Bequests come from monthly donors.** Erica Waasdorp, author of *Monthly Giving: The Sleeping Giant:* "75% of charitable

AS220 invites you to join the movement as we build a creative community committed to the values of access, equity, and social justice!

How a $2.26 Thanksgiving meal can open the door to change

With every meal costing just $2.26, you'll never know the impact you can make. Just ask Norman …

THIS IS THE KIND OF IMPACT YOU CAN MAKE AT THANKSGIVING

"The Mission taught me how to be a man. How to be responsible. And what true love is. The people I met there have become like family."
—Norman

DONATE NOW

Before coming to the Mission, Norman's life was a mess.

"I was smoking meth and doing heroin," he says. "And it cost me everything. My family, my friends, my cars, a place to live. I didn't have anywhere to go."

Then someone told Norman about Nashville Rescue Mission. "You can stay there, they'll feed you, and they have showers," he was told.

With nothing to lose, he came for lunch and unknowingly sat down beside one of our counselors. Seeing the hurt in Norman's eyes, the counselor told him, "We have a program for you."

AS220 is well known to the arts-minded in Providence, Rhode Island. This busy, sprawling arts group (it started with a budget of $800 in 1985 and by 2018 owned three large, renovated buildings) has contributed significantly to the downtown revitalization of this particular post-industrial city—once the richest place on earth, now struggling economically. Expert Erica Waasdorp recommends a very low entry-level price point for monthly giving. Her view: get as many donors in the door as you can; you can always upgrade them later. A low initial gift amount is the practice of power-fundraiser, Nashville Rescue Mission, as you see in this 2018 email solicitation.

bequests now come from monthly donors. A bequest is 7 times more likely from a monthly donor."

- **It kills fewer trees.** Most of your donor communications are handled electronically, not with paper.

- **Inertia works in your favor.** It takes time and trouble to cancel an automated payment. Most people don't bother. True confession: I'm still giving to charities years after my infatuation with them died. Don't get me wrong: they still do important work. But if I weren't so lazy, I'd dump them for some other cause.

- **Monthly donors get "high on giving" 12 times a year**, rather than just once. In chapter 4, you heard about the "happiness chemicals" that make philanthropy such a pleasure. I have experienced this myself. I've come to *prefer* monthly giving to annual giving; it's chemically more rewarding.

CHAPTER 24

Why donors quit

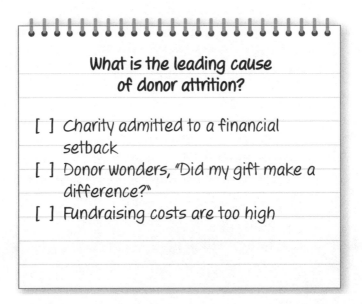

What is the leading cause
of donor attrition?

[ ] Charity admitted to a financial
setback
[ ] Donor wonders, "Did my gift make a
difference?"
[ ] Fundraising costs are too high

D on't fear your donors. They really *do* want to help. They derive pleasure from helping: recall the three "happiness chemicals." Plus they're shockingly forgiving of your foibles (up to a point).

One thing you should realize, though: donors are not giving TO you. They're giving THROUGH you, to make something important happen. Screw your head on straight. From your donors' point of view, your charity is a means to an end . . . and *merely* a means to that end.

Richard Perry co-founded the fabled Domain Group, a large full-service fundraising agency. He then went on to found the Veritas Group, a major-gifts consultancy with an astounding record.

For more than forty years, Richard has obsessively studied donor retention: why they arrive, why they stay, why they leave. His conclusion? "The greatest cause of donor attrition is that the donor did not know she made a difference."

Over and over in donor surveys, you hear the same complaint: "I have no idea what they did with my money."

This is a simple problem to fix. You report to your donors, usually via newsletters. As Steven Screen and Jim Shapiro of The Better Fundraising Company explain, "She sees how her gift made a difference. She feels great, trusts your organization, and is more likely to give again."

Stephen Pidgeon built and eventually sold a major UK direct mail fundraising agency called Tangible. In his 2015 "everything I know" advice book, *How to Love Your Donors (to Death)*, he makes this point: "It is the fundraiser's job, your only job, to make the supporter feel good about supporting your charity. You have to love your donors. The money will follow."

CHAPTER 25

"That's so 2003"

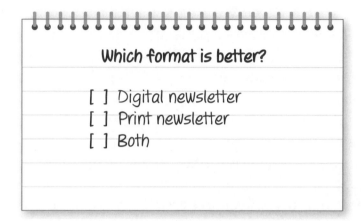

That was the year I first heard the question raised by a fundraiser in a workshop.

She asked, "When can we retire our print donor newsletter and switch to an emailed version instead?"

I didn't know the answer until at least a decade later. And the answer was, "For now, you have to do both, if you want to maximize income and impact."

We are in a transition period. Multichannel communications are the rule for now and the foreseeable future. In 2018, Mark Phillips, Bluefrog's founder, shared data showing the bending seven-year trend in the UK:

- purely "offline" donors (i.e., donors who used the mail to make their gifts) *had* decreased—although at 89.4 percent, they were *still* the vast majority;

- purely online donors (i.e., donors who reacted to an email and gave via a website) were increasing—almost doubling in number in the past three years;

- and "multichannel" donors were becoming a new normal.

What exactly is *multichannel*? Someone receives a direct mail appeal. It prompts her to make a gift . . . but they make that gift online. Or someone sees a text-to-give poster in the subway . . . and takes action via his mobile.

Both are examples of print and digital working together.

In hindsight, 1995 was such a simple time. The internet was just beginning to shoulder its way into our lives. If you knew how traditional print channels worked, you were fine.

Today, effective communicators have to know both print and digital . . . and that will almost certainly remain the case at least until baby boomers pass from this earth and infants have internet connectivity inserted at birth.

CHAPTER 26

If donors enjoy what you're saying

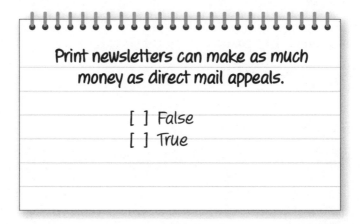

Print newsletters can make as much
money as direct mail appeals.

[ ] False
[ ] True

"Years of meager returns show that printed charity newsletters are a waste of money. They are a cost, not a profit, center," so the Senior Management Team reports. "We should switch to something emailed. About time, too. No one reads print these days. Email is cheaper, faster, and just as good."

So goes the conventional thinking.

And it's wrong. Take, for example, the Nashville Rescue Mission, "a Christ-centered community seeking to help the hurting of Middle Tennessee."

Every $1 the Mission spends on publishing and mailing its monthly printed newsletter yields almost $7 in gifts—a gilded return on investment (ROI) of nearly 700 percent. In a typical year, the mission's print newsletter alone will account for $2 million in gifts, many of them completed online.

Is Nashville's seven-to-one ROI a fluke? It's on the high side, true. But it's far from a fluke. Nashville is yet one more example of a competent donor newsletter built atop the Domain Formula.

In the 1990s, Seattle's Domain Group, already one of America's more successful fundraising agencies, tested the elements of a printed donor newsletter. Like most of us, they pretty much assumed that print newsletters were a waste of money and time.

To their surprise, they found that a charity could **make just as much money from a newsletter as it could from its appeals**, assuming that charity followed certain rules. (It was close, mind you. But newsletters beat appeals by a nose.) As the Domain Group reported:

- Competent printed newsletters sent to current donors raise $3.33 for every dollar spent (on printing, postage, overhead and other costs).

- Competent direct mail appeals sent to current donors raise $3.22 for every dollar spent.

Counter-intuitive? Yes. Magic? No.

Done properly, newsletters and appeals have equal pulling power. The take-away? Do as many as you can . . . of both.

What exactly *is* the Domain Formula . . . and how do you properly apply it? As it happens, there's a book about that.

There are surprises. Did you know, for instance, that mailing a donor newsletter *in an envelope* raises far more money than sending the very same donor newsletter *as a self-mailer*? Here's the data, supplied by Jeff Brooks in 2013:

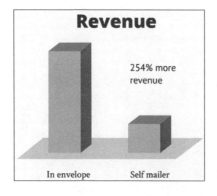

Revenue

254% more revenue

In envelope   Self mailer

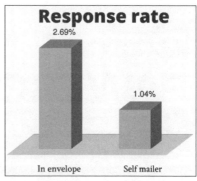

Response rate

2.69%

1.04%

In envelope   Self mailer

Average gift

$54.36

$39.82

In envelope   Self mailer

In 2012, Bob Ball, SVP and creative director at Masterworks, a superb agency specializing in faith-based charities, wrote, "Over the years, I've seen a lot of different kinds of newsletters from non-profit organizations. Some simply report accomplishments. Others are nothing more than fundraising appeals, thinly disguised in newsletter clothing. Still, others are institutionally-focused pieces written for insiders.

"One of the most effective types is the **Extreme Donor-Focused Newsletter**. It is aimed squarely at the donor. In fact, it is all ABOUT the donor.

"This approach assumes donors give because they love to give and love to make a significant difference in the world. It combines reporting back about what the donors have accomplished, and offers them a clear opportunity to give again."

Humane Society
of Northeast Georgia

SPRING 2018

PAWESOME POST

Sharing the life-saving difference you make every day for our homeless rescue friends!

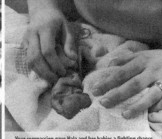

Your compassion gave Nala and her babies a fighting chance

Contact Us

The Humane Society
of Northeast Georgia
845 West Ridge Road
Gainesville, GA 30501

Adoption Center is open:
Tues-Sat 10-5 and Sunday 12-5

Wellness Clinic is open:
Tues-Fri 10-4 and the first Saturday
of each month 9-3

**Spay/neuter surgery and intakes
are by appointment only**

Table of Contents

A Fight for Life:
How You Were This Family's Hero

What started as a routine rescue quickly became a fight for life for a stray mama and her unborn babies.

Thanks to your support, earlier this year HSNEGA rescued a very pregnant mama, Nala, who'd been wandering the streets, eating from garbage cans and sleeping under random porches.

Nala went to a foster home to await delivery. Days went by with no babies, so Nala had x-rays which showed 10 puppies! The number of babies was concerning since Nala is only 20 pounds, so round-the-clock monitoring began.

More days passed, and still no signs of labor, but the babies started going into distress so the HSNEGA team performed an emergency c-section. Miraculously, all the babies were alive when taken from Nala, but that's when their fight really began.

Sadly, Nala was unable to produce milk to keep 10 puppies alive, and even with bottle feeding round-the-clock, six babies wound up passing away within a few days. The deck was simply stacked against this family after a life of neglect. A rescue partner experienced in bottle-feeding newborns stepped in to take the remaining four babies while Nala went back to foster care to heal from her surgery and broken heart.

Nala's story... abandoned mamas fighting to live and protect their babies... is one we see again and again, but with your support, future "Nalas" will always have a fighting chance! Thank you for being their life-saving hero!

The Humane Society of Northeast Georgia mails a print newsletter to donors twice a year. The donor is warmly thanked in the headline and repeatedly in this cover story. Executive director Julie Edwards reported, "Our team decided to 'overhaul' our bi-annual newsletter, making it more donor-centric and visually appealing (more photos, color, etc.) following a 'newsletter audit' by Agents of Good. The results have been incredible. . . . we exceeded our spring goal for donations from the newsletter by 40%!"

As a duly diligent agency, Masterworks ran statistically valid tests. Their tests showed that the "Extreme Donor-Focused Newsletter":

- Improved response to the newsletter 419 percent

- Increased the average gift prompted by the newsletter 19.5 percent

For

- A total boost in charitable revenue at year end of 521 percent

You might want to print those test results out, to hang over your desk as a reminder.

This delightful (and seasonal; in the original, it's an autumn shot in full color) newsletter envelope delivers joy and affirmation immediately to BNRC member/donors. Berkshire Natural Resources Council recently completed its first-ever capital campaign ahead of schedule and above goal. Why? In part because, under the leadership of long-time ED Tad Ames, their communications warmly embraced donor-centricity . . . and donors responded.

How many pages should your print newsletter be?

"Here's something weird," Jeff Brooks noted in November 2018. "In newsletter testing, 8-page newsletters have consistently under-performed 4-page newsletters; you spend more to raise less. And 2-pagers (that is, one sheet, front and back) usually do just as well as 4 . . . you spend less to raise the same."

CHAPTER 27

Putting statistics in their place

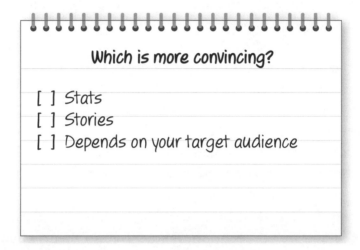

Which is more convincing?

[ ] Stats
[ ] Stories
[ ] Depends on your target audience

Certain funding sources insist on statistical reporting: government agencies and big foundations, to name the obvious. And they have the specialists to digest the data you submit.

With individual donors, though, it's different. Now you're talking brain chemistry. Here's Professor Paul J. Zak writing in the *Harvard Business Review*, in an October 28, 2014, article titled, "Why Your Brain Loves Good Storytelling":

> Many business people have already discovered the power of storytelling in a practical sense—they have observed how compelling a well-constructed narrative can be. But recent scientific work is putting a much finer point on just how stories change our attitudes, beliefs, and behaviors. . . .

By taking blood draws before and after the narrative, we found that character-driven stories do consistently cause oxytocin synthesis. [Oxytocin is a neurochemical that motivates us to cooperate.] Further, the amount of oxytocin released by the brain predicted how much people were willing to help others; for example, donating money to a charity associated with the narrative.

Storytelling produces oxytocin. Statistics don't.

The whole "statistics vs. stories" debate is kind of pointless anyway. And yet it's harder to kill than an urban legend. The average person assumes: "Some people like stories. Some people like numbers." Stories, numbers: even-steven.

But even-steven is nowhere near the truth . . . when you're talking to individual donors.

Correctly, it should be stated: "ALL individual donors like stories"—as you've seen, there's feel-good neurochemistry involved—"and a few individual donors can appreciate numbers as well."

That's the brain's true state. Storytelling—narrative, if you prefer a fancier name—is universal. It has been more important to human evolution than opposable thumbs, as Lisa Cron points out in her excellent book, *Wired for Story: The Writer's Guide to Using Brain Science to Hook Readers from the Very First Sentence.*

Emotions totally rule

In a contest between two appeals for the same charity, one logical and well reasoned vs. one that's packed with emotional hooks . . . well, it's not really a contest.

The *emotional* appeal will bring in far more donations than will the *rational* appeal. Every time. Guaranteed. Because of the brain's hard wiring.

With the advent of Functional MRIs and other investigative tools in the late twentieth century, neuroscientists were finally able to directly observe a phenomenon they'd suspected for more than a century: the dominance of emotion in human decision making.

As USC neuroscientist Dr. Antoine Bechara sums it up, "There is a popular notion, which most of us learn from early on in life, that logical, rational calculation forms the basis of sound decisions. Many people say, 'emotion has no IQ'; emotion can only cloud the mind and interfere with good judgment. But . . . these notions [are] wrong and [have] no scientific basis." Instead, "decision-making is a process guided by emotions."

As the *New York Times* reported back in 2007, "A bevy of experiments in recent years suggest that the conscious mind is like a monkey riding a tiger of subconscious decisions and actions in progress, frantically making up stories about being in control."

Now hear this: emotion leads to action

Making a gift to charity is an act. It's an act prompted by empathy, desire, pleasure, anger, or a host of other emotions (psychologists have delineated more than one hundred states in the human emotional pantry).

Here's the problem: reason bangs on exactly the wrong door, if action is your goal.

Neurological researcher Donald B. Calne famously explained it this way: "The essential difference between emotion and reason is that emotion leads to action while reason leads to conclusions."

In other words, your charity's well-reasoned argument might get me *thinking*. But it's your ability to touch my emotions that gets me *giving*. That's why professional copywriters always lead with emotion in their appeals to individual donors . . . and *then* drag in some reason; not the reverse.

Direct mail writer Tina Cincotti summed up the science nicely. "People act because you moved them emotionally—you made them feel something. MRIs show that it's our brain's emotional nerve center that gets activated first. It's not a rational, logical process where we weigh costs against benefits and make an informed decision. Your brain gets involved later, largely as a rubber stamp to make sure you don't do anything too wacky! But it starts with the heart. If you're not hitting your donors on an emotional level, then you're not raising as much money as you could."

International marketing guru Seth Godin agrees. "Marketers don't convince. Engineers convince. Marketers persuade. Persuasion appeals to the emotions and to fear and to the imagination. Convincing requires a spreadsheet or some other rational device. If you're spending a lot of your time trying to convince people, it's no wonder it's not working."

Stories sell. Statistics tell.

Stories are for everyone. Statistics are for specialists.

Stories need no translation. Statistics do.

Beware big numbers, too

Joseph Stalin said it memorably: "One man's death is a tragedy. A thousand deaths is a statistic."

Psychologist Paul Slovic has coined the term for the phenomenon: "psychic numbing." His research found that big numbers tend to *reduce* response; as a consequence, not as many people jump to help. Behavioral economist Dan Ariely at Duke confirmed the same result. "People give half as much to [hungry]Africa as they give to a hungry girl [in Africa]."

"Most people are caring and will exert great effort," Professor Slovic wrote, "to rescue individual victims whose needy plight comes to their attention. These same good people, however, often become numbly indifferent to the plight of individuals who are 'one of many.'"

Why? He concluded, "The reported numbers of deaths represent dry statistics, 'human beings with the tears dried off,' that fail to spark emotion or feeling and thus fail to motivate action."[1]

When you communicate with individual donors—whether it's in your appeals, newsletters, website, emails, Facebook postings—you should favor stories, not stats. Jeff Brooks, writing in Future Fundraising Now on January 12, 2016, says:

Here are some common mistakes [adopted from PhilanTopic] that drain emotion from messages:

Mistakenly assume that every person is an expert.

Ignore the emotional appeal of their brand.

Put too much emphasis on the "investment."

Try to sell an idea instead of impact.

Think you can instruct people into caring.

Think emotion is somehow dishonestly manipulative.

Your primary goal is to feel good about what you say and how you say it.

"Dignity" is extremely important to you.

Political correctness.

Jeff concludes, "Fundraising that works is emotional. It's simplistic, blatant, corny, and soupy. That's just the way it is. There's

1   Paul Slovic, "'If I Look at the Mass I Will Never Act: Psychic Numbing and Genocide," *Judgment and Decision Making* 2, no.2 (April 2007): 79. Dr. Slovic is a professor of psychology at the University of Oregon and the president of Decision Research.

nothing wrong with your donors. That's just the playground you're playing on when you do fundraising."

You will encounter staff who feel that "simplistic, blatant, corny, and soupy" fundraising is somehow manipulative, even unethical. They are wrong (if loud and persistent). And their personal opinions may be dangerous to your fundraising's bottom line if you cave to them (so don't).

CHAPTER 28

Is ignorance a barrier to giving?

"We need to educate our donors."

[ ] True
[ ] False

The presumption goes something like this: *New donors come in pretty uninformed about our important work. If we can teach them more about it, they'll come to admire it, understand it, and hence contribute more.*

So authorities teach.

While unaware donors presumably learn.

Which usually ends up being (put yourself in your donors' shoes for a moment) boring, irrelevant or condescending.

The special features of your programs are *not* why donors remain loyal. Program details are fascinating to insiders: staff, board, maybe volunteers. To donors?

Here's the plain, unsubtle truth: *if* your organization *could* cure cancer, end homelessness, put poverty behind us, empower girls and feed the hungry with a magic wand, that would be just fine, thank you. Outsiders (synonym: all your donors) would be delighted. Donors will now and forever happily *fund* your magic wands.

Insiders and outsiders

Accept that downgrade, insiders.

In donors' eyes, magic wands are just as good as your wonderful programs . . . maybe even better!

Insiders care about *how* it works . . . just as old-time watchmakers cared about mainsprings, gears, balance wheels and escapements.

Outsiders just want to know, "What time is it?" Outsiders care about impact: i.e., *did* it work? *Did* something change "thanks to my gift"?

Donors don't need to remember the name of the program. They don't need to know how it's staffed. They don't need to know the underlying philosophy. All they really need to know is that you have an *effective* program.

Accept this humble precept: "How the organization functions is irrelevant to our donors. Our impact is the only thing that really counts."

As said previously, people aren't giving *to* you. They're giving *through* you, to make something happen, a point superstar fundraising consultant Tom Suddes has been making for years.

Connect with what's already in their heads

Richard Radcliffe, cited before, is a UK-based researcher.

He's personally interviewed more than twenty-five thousand donors (and counting), asking them about their deeper motivations for giving. His conclusion? "Donors are spectacularly ignorant of the causes they support."

But he didn't mean that was a bad thing. On the contrary; he meant, "Lucky us!" We don't have to explain very much to win someone's support for our cause.

Donors may be "ignorant" of how a charity does its work. But donors have in abundance their own personal values, interests, beliefs, connections, experiences, upbringing, lost loves, secret passions, regrets, fears, angers, hopes and built-in empathy.

Rather than educate donors about your work, take them on a journey.

Ditch the data and the dry details. Tell stories instead. When you take donors on a never-ending journey to witness fascinating (or appalling) things, donors tend to remain with a cause longer, Adrian Sargeant's research has found.

Educating insiders

"Educating our donors" is not a road to riches.

But there *is* a type of education that matters a lot to a nonprofit's growth and sustainability.

If your nonprofit depends on gifts to keep its doors open, it is vitally important to educate *insiders* (senior management, staff, board, volunteers) about the role of philanthropy in your organization's mission.

I had a client that was 88 percent dependent on philanthropy to fund its $20 million annual operating budget . . . and yet even the CFO seemed unaware of this fact. That kind of "insider ignorance" will definitely lead to missteps and misunderstandings.

CHAPTER 29

"The difference between anger and compassion is huge"

For an animal welfare charity, which will raise more money?

[ ] Stories of animal rescues and adoptions
[ ] Stories of cruelty to animals

It was puzzling . . . and costly.

In just six years, an obviously competent (in fact, amazingly wonderful) US-based animal-welfare charity saw more than 30 percent of its annual donors stop giving.

There is, of course, normal donor attrition: people move, lose jobs, die. This, though, was *abnormal*, off-the-charts attrition . . . especially since the charity's direct-mail donor-acquisition program was going great guns, bringing in three times the industry norm.

Why were these same people quitting *so* fast?

An obscure case study conducted in the UK held the answer. Ken Burnett talked about it in a 2010 blog post.[2]

"Alan [Clayton] was working with a major animal welfare organisation. Their direct marketing income from warm[3] appeals was declining. No change in creative technique, copy, or data segmentation seemed capable of halting the decline."

The UK fields some of the world's best and most innovative fundraisers. Ken Burnett is in that tradition. Alan Clayton, a generation younger, is in that tradition.

Alan's charity client then reviewed five years of direct mail appeals. "They soon noticed something very special," Ken reported. "Whenever an appeal featured just animals, it performed poorly; but when it contained stories about bad and good humans as well as animals, it performed well."

Alan Clayton: "The insight we gained from these detailed records was that the feeling that drove action was *anger* at the injustice meted out to animals by cruel humans rather than *compassion* for the animals themselves. So our next appeal featured anger and injustice in a fiery creative treatment. Income *doubled* immediately. It has stayed at the higher level ever since."

Ken Burnett again: "The lesson was that the organisation should communicate as an 'anti-human-cruelty' organisation rather than as a 'save-the-cute-animal' organisation. A fundamentally different way of saying the same thing."

---

2   Ken Burnett, "Bring Back the Indispensable Guard Book," Ken Burnett's website, 2010, http://www.kenburnett.com/BlogGuard%20book.html. Accessed Dec. 4, 2018.

3   "Warm appeals" simply means appeals sent to those who last gave within a year or so. As opposed to "cold."

Sometimes the right case study is a godsend

Let's return to the US-based animal-welfare charity I mentioned at the start. For the past six years, they'd acquired donors thanks to *anger*, i.e., cruelty-horrified appeals. But *then* their donor newsletters only reported happy stories: adoptions, cures, fixes. It was a steady stream of happy endings.

That's a disconnect for donors.

Insiders liked the happy talk instinctively. They didn't want to *upset* anyone. And talking about the gruesome truth of human

Most so-called "readers" read nothing but the headlines, research found. So even skimmers will see that Lollypop Farm's problems are never completely solved: "Luna is learning to love."

cruelty was exhausting and painful . . . for staff *and* donors. And yet the battle against human cruelty led to outsized giving.

Conclusion? Donor newsletters should NOT be ENTIRELY about an organization's or a program's success. Those messages subliminally convince donors you do NOT need their help.

The lizard brain

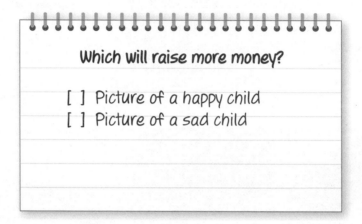

Which will raise more money?

[ ] Picture of a happy child
[ ] Picture of a sad child

This is a question you can easily get both right *and* wrong.

Your gut tells you that sad kids probably raise more money. But then your mind reasons, "Yeah, but if we show real-life happy kids, donors will see that our programs are successful."

Makes perfect sense. Yet it's not even close.

The American Marketing Association's 2011 *Journal of Marketing Research*, reported by Jeff Brooks, found that a photo of a sad child raises 50 percent more than a photo of either a neutral or a happy child.

"Kids like Jenny need heroes like you." That's classic fundraising: you show a child in trouble, and you invite the kind-hearted to help.[4]

There's a biological reason why sad images raise more money.

---

4   Creative by Ask Direct, Dublin.

We all have a lump of neurons popularly called "the lizard brain." It's early software—wired in at the start of the human evolutionary journey. "It is in charge of fight, flight, feeding, fear, freezing-up, and fornication," Dr. Joseph Troncale explains in a 2014 *Psychology Today* article.

When we blinked primordial mud from our eyes, two alarming thoughts dominated our primitive processors. Both were survival messages:

(1) "Can I eat it?" (*I need nutrition.*)
(2) "Will it kill me?" (*It needs nutrition.*)

If undelivered, please return to: Barnárdos, Merchants Hall, 25-26 Merchants Quay, Dublin 8

Postage Paid Postas Íochta	Baile Átha Cliath
DM	Ceadúnas 1452

Kids like Jenny need heroes like you. Barnardos
No child gets left behind

In your modern skull and mine, that original "lizard brain" has become what science calls the *amygdala* (pronounced "ah-MIG-duh-la," named for its almond-ish shape).

"Shown to play a key role in the processing of emotions, the amygdala [a cluster of neurons] . . . is linked to both fear responses

THE SAD-HAPPY STORY CYCLE

ASK
Sad Stories

THANK
Happy Stories

REMIND
Happy and Sad Stories

and pleasure," ScienceDaily says.[5] As NYU neuroscientist Joseph LeDoux states in *Emotionomics*, "Negative emotions are linked to survival—and are much stronger."

See something calming, like a child's smile? Relax. No worries.

See something dangerous, like a typical front-page news story? The lizard brain issues an abrupt order: PAY ATTENTION NOW!

Why *does* daily journalism dwell so much on disasters, murders, slaughters, catastrophes and other insults to your peace of mind?

Because your lizard brain says YOU MUST PAY ATTENTION . . . which means, in turn, your for-profit news entity of choice can then sell your eyeballs to its advertisers.

---

5   Here's a fun fact: "[The amygdala's] size is positively correlated with aggressive behavior across species. In humans, it . . . shrinks by more than 30% in males upon castration." Food for thought, peaceniks.

A Letter from Home

VIDA JOVEN DE MÉXICO

A Newsletter for You from the Children of Vida Joven

Daniel, 3rd grade, does his homework at Vida Joven. Favorite school tool? Scissors

4 MILLION SCHOOL-AGE KIDS IN MEXICO DEPRIVED OF EDUCATION*

THANKS TO YOU, 8-year-old Daniel isn't one of them

It's scary to think what Daniel's life would be like if he didn't have your support. You're making a big difference for him. Huge, really.

You see, Daniel probably wouldn't be in school if you weren't on his side. Poverty is the biggest reason children and teens don't attend school in Mexico.

Now, look again at Daniel's face.

That smile you see? He went to school today. It's a public school right around the corner from the orphanage. Daniel has a teacher who cares about him.

When Daniel got home from school today, he ate a big, healthy lunch. After lunch, Daniel called out to one of the Vida Joven staff, "Yolanda! Will you help me with my homework?"

Because of you, this kid went to school today. Because of you, he came home to a delicious lunch. Because of you, Daniel had homework assistance from caring adults at the orphanage.

That smile on his face? **BECAUSE OF YOU!!**

P.S. Daniel needs your continued help so he can keep going to school. Your gift of $22 will cover his educational expenses for two weeks: www.VJGive.org

Source: UNICEF 2017

Founded in 1996 by people from the San Diego–Los Angeles area, Vida Joven ("young lives") is an orphanage in Tijuana, Mexico. I'm a donor. Their newsletter brings me so much joy . . . and takes me on an intimate, revealing journey to a place I'll probably never visit in person.

HOMEWORK, HOMEWORK, LOTS OF HOMEWORK...

These kids don't know how lucky they are! Thanks to you, they don't have to worry about where they'll sleep. Or what they'll eat.

They don't have to worry whether they'll be loved and protected. Instead, they GET to do homework every day. All because you care.

It takes Diana a l-o-n-g time to finish her homework. But she always finishes! Favorite school tool? Colored pencils

Kevin used to need lots of homework assistance. Now he's working more independently. Favorite school tool? Mechanical pencil.

Verania is in 9th grade. And she's university-bound, thanks to your support. Favorite school tool? English-Spanish dictionary.

Karla crosses every "t" and dots every "i." (Firstborn child!) Favorite school tool? Post-it notes.

Carolina is quite the math whiz. Favorite school tool? A thick eraser.

Page 2

Graphic design discounted by VIVID Digital Design.
Printing discounted by Replica Printing.

Steven Screen, principal at Seattle-based The Better Fundraising Co., follows this simple guideline: use negative imagery in your appeals; use positive imagery in your newsletters. Online guru John Haydon, author of *Facebook for Dummies*, offers a useful variant on the same idea:

Many nonprofits wish they could abandon negative imagery altogether, even when asking.

It's a well-meaning instinct. But it will likely have a downside.

In one recent test I saw, a large US charity removed all the sad images and messages from an appeal that had previously been successful, inserting happy images and messages instead. Result? Response rates fell 10 percent, bringing in 17 percent less revenue. Happy faces don't trigger empathy, a powerful precursor to giving.

But happy faces in newsletters *do* reassure the donor that progress is happening.

CHAPTER 31

Faster

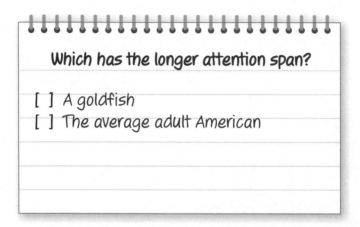

Which has the longer attention span?

[ ] A goldfish
[ ] The average adult American

S cience measures such things.

In 2003, the average adult American had a longer attention span than the goldfish. A decade later, things had reversed. By 2013, the goldfish was #1. You can do this test at home. If you have a goldfish, stare into the bowl. See which of you breaks eye contact first.

So what happened between 2003 and 2013?

- In 2004, Mark Zuckerberg and his roommate introduced Facebook as a Harvard exclusive; by 2006, anyone with an email address could join. "As of the second quarter of 2018," Statista reported, "Facebook had 2.23 billion monthly active users." Users spend an average of twenty minutes per day looking at Facebook.

- In 2007, Apple unveiled the iPhone. The large touchscreen proved popular. By 2017, Apple had sold almost 217 million of the addictive devices. As the *New York Post* reported in 2017, "A study by . . . Asurion found that the average person struggles to go little more than 10 minutes without checking their phone. And of the 2,000 people surveyed, one in 10 check their phones on average once every four minutes."

Smashed to smithereens in the process? Your attention span. My attention span. Everyone's attention span . . . including donors and prospective donors.

Is this cause for alarm? No. It's cause for consideration. We're heading ever deeper into the Age of Constant Distraction. You can't fight it. You have to work with it.

What to do in self-defense?

Get faster, at the very least.

The first few seconds

We all suffer from information overload.

"Every two days now we create as much information as we did from the dawn of civilization up until 2003," Google CEO Eric Schmidt told a conference in 2010. That's the big picture.

What's it like for you and me personally? A study conducted by researchers at the University of California San Diego estimated that, between digital and print sources, the equivalent of 174 newspapers' worth of information are aimed at our brains . . . daily. And that was in 2007.

Yet we cope.

We straightaway sort that daily "info-lanche" into three manageable piles.

- Pile #1: Stuff I cannot safely ignore because, if I do, something bad will happen to me. (Bills, a jury-duty summons, an email from my sister.)

- Pile #2: Stuff I *can* safely ignore and *nothing* bad will happen to me. (This pile includes all your attempts to communicate with me.)

- Pile #3: A few items extracted from pile #2 because they interest me for some reason. I'll put those items aside for a second look. On your best days, your stuff *might* make it into pile #3.

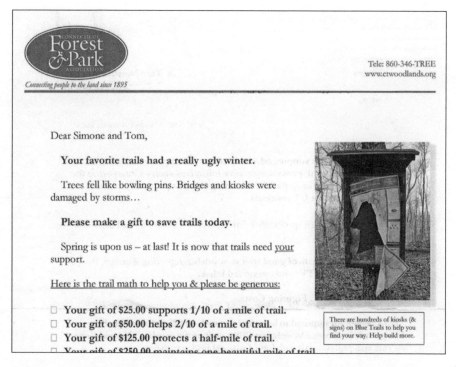

This appeal starts blazingly fast. It's personal immediately: "Your favorite trails had a really ugly winter." Gives me a couple of quick visuals ("bowling pins" and a photo of a storm-damaged kiosk) to fill in the blanks. Then makes its first ask just twenty words in.

Nonprofit communications do not enjoy special status. In fact, they're common as dirt . . . and getting more common all the time as the charity sector grows. Your messages, particularly your fundraising messages, are part of the onslaught. In my world, you are an intrusion . . . even when I'm a loyal donor.

Please remain acutely aware: each time you attempt to communicate with me, my first gift to you *won't* be my money.

My first gift to you will be a moment or two of my precious attention.

CHAPTER 32

Organization-focused vs. donor-focused

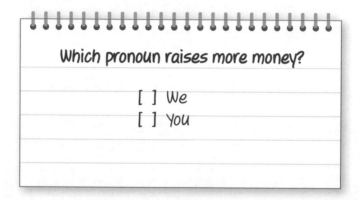

"We need you!"

It's efficient: two pronouns; one verb (the call to action); an exclamation point; and inescapable eye contact with a finger-pointing British Secretary of State for War, Lord Kitchener, in 1914 a revered imperial icon of military masculinity.

This blunt recruiting message helped mobilize 6 million British troops in World War One; 600,000 then died in the conflict.

So, what do *you* think? *Which* of the two pronouns did the most to move young men to enlist? Hint: the winner's the one in bigger type.

The word "you" is different. It's not just a pronoun. It's more like a sudden hand clap. Merely mentioning "you" *forces* my brain—and yours—to pay more attention automatically, without our consent.

The word "you" makes *everything* suddenly personal.

Your fundraising success will depend on how you talk

There are two ways you can talk to your "base" (your current and potential donors, members, supporters, volunteers, etc.).

Way #1 is organization-centered: "We do this amazing program. We do that amazing program. Oh, by the way, if you have sent in a gift, thanks!"

Way #2 is donor-centered: "With your help, all these amazing programs happen. And without your help, they are not possible."

The big difference is which comes first, "we" or "you."

Here's my promise, backed by solid recent research and years of experience: when "you" comes first, you'll raise more money. When "we" comes first, you'll raise less.

In one experiment, donations to a children's hospital foundation skyrocketed 1,000 percent when its newsletter changed the way it talked.

When the newsletter *stopped* bragging first and foremost about the excellence of the medicine and *switched* instead to talking about what a difference donors made in the lives of sick kids, contributions per issue leaped from $5,000 to $50,000.

That $50,000 in gifts per issue became this newsletter's new normal. In the decade that followed, the foundation's newsletter brought in $2 million in donations. If it had stuck to its old way of talking, it would have raised merely $200,000 over the same period.

The psychology's not complicated: when you're nice to me, I'll be nice back. Dr. Robert Cialdini calls the phenomenon "reciprocity." It's one of his famous "Six Principles of Persuasion."

Assume you're doing it wrong

I've analyzed thousands of appeals, websites, newsletters, social media, thanks, invitations, annual reports, videos, etc. from

Jeff Brooks calls it "the Batman Model." It's not the model you want. "Batman is the Boss. Robin is the helper, the sidekick. Batman gets all the glory. And a way cooler costume. The Batman Model puts the organization in the starring role. The donor is the helper whose donations help enable the work. Batman fundraising is full of phrases like 'Please donate so we can . . .', 'Help us help the children . . .', 'Support this great work. . . .'" Reprinted from the Future Fundraising Now blog.

countless charities across the US, Canada, Australia, New Zealand, the UK and Ireland.

In much of what I see, nonprofits choose to speak in way #1. The charity comes first, the donor comes last. The charity's work dominates, the donor's contribution is nice but subordinate.

As a fundraising tactic, hogging the credit (way #1) limits your success. You'll gather just the lowest of low-hanging fruit. If you want the full harvest, you must freely, without restraint and with delighted abandon share the credit with your donors (way #2).

CHAPTER 33

Surprise!

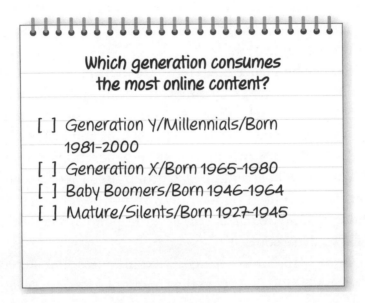

n 2015, the stereotype of the online-addicted millennial[6] failed the real-world test, much to everyone's shock.

In a joint study titled "The Generational Content Gap," Fractl and BuzzStream surveyed a statistically valid sample of Americans regarding their consumption of digital content.

Adweek, the US bible for that industry, reported, "Interestingly, a higher proportion of Baby Boomers spend more [time] per week

---

6   Should we capitalize a generation's name? Even the grammar police aren't sure. Several august authorities (including the Oxford English Dictionary Online and the *AP Stylebook*) say to capitalize Generation X but *not* to capitalize millennial or baby boomer. *Adweek* begs to differ.

consuming online content than either Millennials or Generation X users."

How *much* more time? Baby boomers consume TWICE as much online content as millennials or Gen Xers, the study found.

There were other revelations.

Time of day mattered. "More Boomers prefer to consume content in the early and late morning (5:00 A.M. to noon) rather than any other time of day."

Preference for device mattered. "Boomers prefer desktops and laptops, as do Gen-Xers. Millennials are the biggest users of mobile, but only approximately 25 percent *primarily* [my emphasis] use mobile devices, while most still use desktops and laptops."

And which platforms did different generations use most in 2015? "Around 60 percent of each group uses Facebook to share content. The next most popular network is YouTube." It's an also-ran, though. "Only 10 percent of survey respondents said they used YouTube to share content."

That was 2015. Times change. But don't guess. Our stereotypes aren't always wrong. But often they're out of date or askew.

CHAPTER 34

What comes first matters

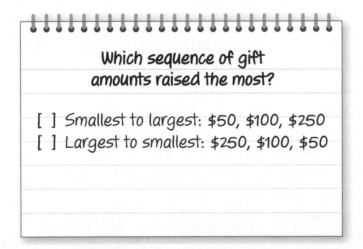

Which sequence of gift
amounts raised the most?

[ ] Smallest to largest: $50, $100, $250
[ ] Largest to smallest: $250, $100, $50

F undraisers call it an "ask string."

You see it in direct mail appeals. It's that set of proposed gift amounts printed on the reply form. Lots of website giving pages offer ask strings, too.

So: which gift string do you think brought in the most money? Was it the largest-to-smallest sequence . . . or the smallest to largest?

Fundraisers in my audiences overwhelmingly guess that the ask string that starts with the *biggest* amount—$250—will raise the most.

And they're wrong.

Actually, in this particular test, the largest-to-smallest ask string raised 25 percent **LESS**. The largest-to-smallest gift array, in fact, was a **TWO-time** loser: not only were fewer gifts made, but the average gift was also smaller.[7]

Now consider this ask string:

$1,000, $500, $250, $100, $50, $25

This ask string comes from the website of a small-town hospice. It's soliciting monthly gifts. It appears in that order, largest to smallest.

I was gobsmacked. Astounded. Flabbergasted.

Why would an ask string seeking *monthly* gifts start with an implausible amount like $1,000, which almost no one can afford? A more typical monthly amount might be $5 or $10 or $20.

One veteran fundraiser had a plausible excuse.

"I was always told to start with the biggest number," she said, "especially in face-to-face solicitations of potential major donors. With them, you don't want to aim too low. You might have gotten twice as much just by asking."

OK; fair enough for major gifts. But why would you apply that same rule of thumb to monthly giving?

There's a name for this in psychology: "magical thinking." It describes an irrational belief. "If we ask for a thousand bucks a month right up front, maybe somebody will do it!"

That's the *least* likely outcome. The *most* likely outcome is you'll simply discourage a lot of people from giving.

Anchoring

We make a lot of decisions using mental shortcuts.

One is called "anchoring." Two Israeli psychologists, Daniel Kahneman and Amos Tversky, deeply explored the phenomenon

---

7   From npENGAGE, reported May 2018 by Future Fundraising Now

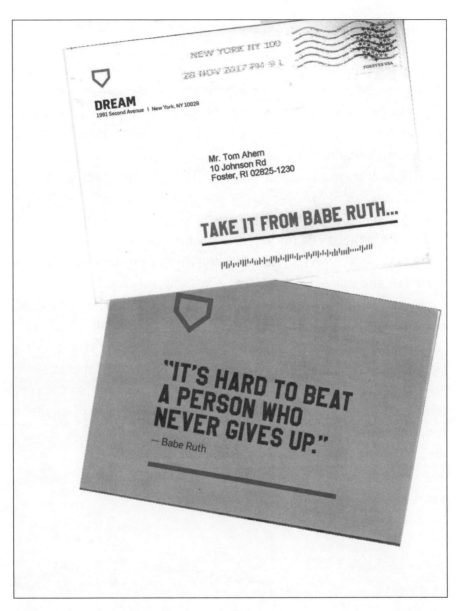

The sole purpose of a fundraising envelope is to "get opened." With the right crowd (New Yorkers, New York Yankee diehards, people over a certain age or their off-spring), Babe Ruth might release that impulse to open.

during the 1970s; later, Kahneman won the 2002 Nobel Prize, in part for this work.

Participants in an early Kahneman/Tversky study were asked to compute, *within five seconds*, the product of the numbers 1 through 8, presented either as $1 \times 2 \times 3 \times 4 \times 5 \times 6 \times 7 \times 8$ or reversed as $8 \times 7 \times 6 \times 5 \times 4 \times 3 \times 2 \times 1$. There wasn't enough time to do the math. Participants had to guess.

When the number 1 started the list, people guessed *low*—a median answer of 512. When the number 8 started the list, people guessed *far higher*—a median answer of 2,250.[8]

Now you basically understand anchoring.

Anchoring[9] more or less explains why the sequence that began with $50 and ended with $250 raised more money.

When people encountered $250 first, they concluded, "Well, that's not me." Either they felt they couldn't afford that big a gift. Or they felt the charity wasn't worth that amount of risk. So they chose not to give at all. On the other hand, when they encountered $50 first, they felt, "Well, OK, I guess I can afford that." Or they felt, "It's a risk. I don't know these people. But at that price, I can take a chance."

---

8 The correct answer is 40,320.
9 "Anchoring" deserves far more attention than I give it here. The Wikipedia article is a good start, if you wish to dig deeper.

CHAPTER 35

Prioritizing

A university fundraiser asked, "In a billion-dollar campaign case, where do you place the 'Letter from the Dean'?"

There's no right answer. There *is* a trite answer: stick it in front. Dean, president, CEO, executive director and/or board chair: "The boss leads the parade." That's the default, ninety-nine times out of one hundred.

Of course, bear in mind that "the way it's always been done" might mean nothing more than: "We have no idea, but everyone else seems to do it this way."

Build success backwards from your target audience

Where is a strong statement from the boss most persuasive? Beginning, middle, end . . . or maybe nowhere?

You run into these questions all the time: in annual reports, newsletters, capital campaign cases, appeals, websites, even events.

Should the boss kick things off? Deliver a big finish? Add heat to a cooling middle? Or maybe stay completely out of it?

It's actually a two-part question:

- *Answer this first:* Will the boss deliver a strong, stirring, challenging, emotionally competent, wake-up, urgent, call-to-action-now message?

- *Then:* If the boss prefers NOT to deliver that kind of strong message, why are you wasting your reader/listener's precious attention on jargon-muddled, bland, predictable, "everything's-great!" PR horse turds?

See how easy it is to decide? You just have to be painfully honest for about five seconds. We've talked about this before. (Remember the goldfish?)

Your target audience has a disposable attention span you can measure in a couple of ticks of the clock. Will you waste that tiny window of opportunity (and disappoint them) by serving up weak, risk-free, utterly safe, emotionally blithering, harmless, forgettable, zero-call-to-action messages?

Your decision.

Selling the threat, selling the promise: If it worked for Yale . . .

Donors wonder, *Why now? Why is this appeal so urgent?*

Sometimes the answer is: "If we don't do it now, things go from bad to worse." Those won't be the exact words used, but that will be the message. I call it "selling the threat, selling the promise." With the right audience, it's irresistible.

VOLUME 4   ISSUE 3   FALL 2016

FACES *of* HOPE

THE DIFFERENCE YOU'RE MAKING FOR NEIGHBORS IN NEED

"I WAS SCARED"

How your gifts gave this
family help and hope

SOCIETY OF ST. VINCENT DE PAUL
HELPING NEIGHBORS STARTS AT HOME

Prioritizing   **147**

How did it do?

The Yale Tomorrow campaign ran from September 2006 to June 30, 2011, slammed by the Great Recession. It raised in total $3.881 billion, stretching well beyond its original goal of $3 billion. "More than 110,000 alumni, parents, friends, corporations, and foundations contributed to the Campaign, directing their gifts to every area of the University," purrs the press release.

But selling the threat by itself isn't enough. Selling the promise is what *really* raises the money. As a case for support, Yale Tomorrow would have been nothing without its comprehensive, far-reaching vision. The threat was there, but merely as a launching pad for a huge leap forward.

CHAPTER 36

Get off the treadmill

Where does most US charity come from?

[ ] Corporations
[ ] Foundations
[ ] Individuals

For more than sixty years, Giving USA has collected reliable data on American generosity. In 2018, the Giving USA foundation released its annual stats for the previous year.

One key measure was no surprise.

As ever, in 2017, individuals contributed most of the charity in America . . . *not* foundations, *not* corporations.

Seventy percent of US giving came from living individuals. Another 9 percent came from dead individuals, via bequests. Another 16 percent came from foundations; individuals probably set up most of those, too. A mere morsel came from corporations: business contributed 5 percent of the US total.

Which begs this question: if you're serious about fundraising, where should you invest your limited time and treasure?

Is your organization serious about the future?

"I see so many small organizations on these never-ending event & grant treadmills," consultant Pam Grow lamented in 2018. She should know: more than twenty thousand nonprofits, mostly small and mid-sized, follow her good advice on Twitter.

Who can attempt event fundraising?

Let's be brutally frank. Anyone who's organized a successful birthday party for a small crowd probably knows "event basics." And who can attempt grant writing?

As far as prerequisites go, anyone who's literate is basically qualified, since few are initially barred from submitting.

Yeah, individuals are tough

There are no shortcuts in fundraising.

Real fundraising, *growth*-oriented fundraising, cannot be done by poorly paid quasi-professionals with a title and no real training. Volunteers, no matter how well intentioned, only get you so far. There are no gimmicks. No asteroids of easy cash will crash through your roof.

Fundraising from individuals is hard work. It requires planning and vision and guts. You think in decades, not months. Everyone pitches in. There is no magic.

If every year your charity faces the same desperate scramble to make ends meet, leadership should look in the mirror.

It's quite possible your *real* problem isn't fundraising. As Simone Joyaux, author of *Strategic Fund Development,* observes: "Probably more than 75% of 'fundraising problems' are not fundraising problems at all. They are organizational development issues—that affect fundraising!"[10]

---

10 Simone Joyaux, *Strategic Fund Development: Building Profitable Relationships That Last,* 3rd ed. (Hoboken, NJ: Wiley, 2011: p. 34.

CHAPTER 37

Swimming in money

Which is your biggest unexploited
fundraising opportunity?

[ ] Charitable bequests
[ ] Facebook fundraising
[ ] Major gifts

I can safely make this promise: if your organization had launched a
competent bequest marketing program ten years ago, today you'd
be swimming in money.

Now, if you answered "Major gifts" rather than "Charitable
bequests," you're not necessarily wrong.

Major gifts—larger gifts from a relatively small number of
people—offer newer *and* smaller organizations an incredibly good
return on their time investment . . . certainly vs. events or grants.
Amy Eisenstein's research, done with Professor Adrian Sargeant
and released in early 2016, found that grants and events cost small
shops anywhere from 20¢ to 50¢ to raise $1, while major gift solici-
tation cost just 10¢ to raise $1: a bargain and a better use of a fun-
draiser's time.

If, however, you're an *established* nonprofit, the road to riches (eventually, anyway) will definitely run through bequests. It's an opportunity few exploit.

I speak to hundreds of fundraisers each year. I'll ask, "How many organizations in this room expect to be out of business in twenty-five years?" No hands go up. Then I ask, "How many of you have an aggressive bequest marketing program?" Again, no hands go up.

Shame.

If you're serious about your organization's sustainability, a solid bequest marketing program is Fundraising 101. (Just ask Harvard University, which now covers something like 43 percent of its annual operating costs from endowment income alone.)

It's cheap and easy to market bequests. It requires one extra letter a year, at a minimum.

Best of all, you don't have to acquire any new donors: your top bequest prospects are ALREADY in your database. They are your truest of true believers: those who've given loyally for years and/or make larger than average annual gifts.

"Tomorrow" dollars? Try three years

One common objection to bequest marketing goes something like this: "Our nonprofit needs money now. There's no point in wasting our fundraiser's precious time on something that won't pay off for another twenty years."

Or even longer, in some cases. Simone and I wrote our first will in our late thirties. It included several gifts to charity. We've amended our will at least twice since then, and those early charitable gifts remain.

"The new average life expectancy for Americans is 78.7 years," *Forbes* magazine reported in 2018. Do the math. If you're one of our favored charities, you'll likely end up waiting forty years before you see our bequest.

But is a forty-year wait typical?

Surprisingly, no.

Those of us who have wills[11] tend to do one last update, as we reach the end of our projected life expectancy. We don't want to leave a mess. And then we die within a couple of years.

Is it worth chasing major gifts that will arrive within one to four years? Most charities would say yes, I imagine.

Well, that is *exactly* the time frame for charitable bequests. Almost half (43 percent) are in the charity's bank account within one to four years of the will's being written or amended. Almost three-quarters (72 percent) of charitable bequests are realized within a decade.[12]

The wait for most bequests isn't long. What are *you* waiting for?

---

11 Something like 60 percent of non-Jewish US households have wills. In US households that *are* Jewish, 74 percent have wills, according to a 2013 study, *Connected to Give*. Will-making varies country to country: in Italy, for instance, I was told that fewer than 10 percent of households have wills, since inheritance laws are clear and strict.

12 Recent research shared by Mark Phillips, founder of London's Bluefrog agency.

Meet Jacqueline

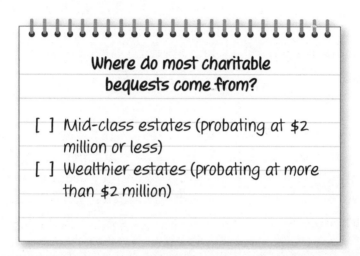

The following bit of vital research appears on page 80 of *Iceberg Philanthropy*. It's part of the profile of "Jacqueline," the "average" North American donor discussed in great detail and depth by this remarkable (and underappreciated) book.

"Jacqueline is typical of those donors who send your organization $35 cheques through the mail. She's the classic ordinary donor. . . . Your major gift officer pays no attention to donors like Jacqueline. Nor does your planned giving officer."[13]

The fact that Jacqueline remains invisible to most nonprofit organizations, even though "she might well have been giving to

---

13 Fraser Green, Ruth McDonald, Jose van Herpt, *Iceberg Philanthropy: Unlocking Extraordinary Gifts from Ordinary Donors* (Ottawa: FLA Group, 2007): 77.

you consistently for 10 or 20 years," means, as *Iceberg Philanthropy* hammers home, that you're probably ignoring most of your best prospects for a bequest.

As Good Works, a fundraising consultancy in Canada, notes, "Legacy marketing . . . is about getting a small number of very large gifts from your 'average' donors. These are the donors who aren't on your radar screen already, who aren't interested in tea and banana bread with a planned giving officer, but who are very loyal to your cause."

More proof?

- The legendary Jerry Panas (1928–2018), founder of Jerold Panas, Linzy & Partners, one of North America's top capital campaign consultancies, in 2016: "It may seem counterintuitive, but actually, those with the greatest net worth are not normally your best or most likely prospects for a bequest.

  "You need to look for men and women who are long term and consistent donors. This is especially true of those who give four or more times a year, several hundred dollars a year. They are your very best prospects for a bequest.

  "The greatest percentage by far are bequests from men and women who leave estates of $2 million or less."

- Kevin Schulman, founder of DonorVoice, also reported in 2016: "The ASPCA asked this question of its database: Who exactly leaves us bequests? The answer: donors who give often but not very much."

- In 2018, Toronto fundraising agency Agents of Good blogged this bit of data, based on extensive research: "Most of your legacy gifts will come from your 'minor' donors . . . that 80% of the file that tends to get ignored."

The truth is, you already know who your best bequest prospects are. They're the donors in your database who give to you faithfully. They're the donors in your database who give you larger than average gifts each year.

You just have to surmount one simple communications obstacle. Asked why they hadn't yet put a gift in their wills, donors will commonly say, "It didn't occur to me to do so."

Make sure it occurs to them. Legacy marketing specialist Richard Radcliffe says the best, basic approach is to mail your bequest prospects a brief letter once a year, reminding them that they can make a spectacular difference by adding a gift in their will.

The case against "planned giving"

US fundraising shops typically categorize charitable bequests as a form of "planned giving."

That's a serious mistake in my view.

It lumps bequests in with a bunch of sophisticated financial products that only the wealthy and their advisors care about or understand.

Nor are planned giving officers (PGOs) the right people to sell bequests.[14] PGOs are technical experts, sometimes lawyers, qualified to explain the arcane tax and income advantages of CRUTs, CRATs, CLATs and Ghoul CLTs. PGOs tend to be reactive, not proactive: when someone makes an inquiry, they respond.

That poor fit, I suspect, is one reason bequest giving in the US perennially and so badly lags bequest giving in the UK and Australia.

---

14 The *right* people to manage bequest marketing are the same people who manage annual giving. Why? Because effective bequest marketing begins with a letter sent once a year to existing donors. PGOs, of course, can do that simple task. They're just not accustomed to doing mass mailings.

In Australia, for example, bequests now account for 17–20 percent of all charity in a given year, more than double what major gifts bring in. In America? In 2017, bequests accounted for 9 percent of all US charity . . . and that was, to my knowledge, a new record; it had puttered along at 7–8 percent for decades.

Stephen Pidgeon devotes chapter 10 of his incisive book, *How to Love Your Donors (to Death)*, to what he terms "legacy marketing." Being a Brit, he doesn't use the term "planned giving." (Nor does Oxford University, by the way, except in one place: in a downloadable PDF titled, "Leaving a bequest to Oxford: Information for US donors.")

And why should anyone in the nonprofit world listen to Stephen Pidgeon? Because he co-founded and ran Tangible, the UK's leading direct mail fundraising agency. When he eventually sold it for a bloody fortune, it had more than four hundred employees.

Here's Stephen's argument, reprinted with permission:

> The sums involved [in legacy marketing] are so huge, the impact of this money is so transforming, that it transcends any other form of fundraising.
>
> All but the biggest major gifts are chicken feed in comparison to legacies. Regular monthly gifts paid through the bank? Legacies dwarf even this welcome source of money. Corporate gifts are but pennies in a bucket.
>
> Yet people in charities (not, thankfully, the fundraisers) don't take legacy marketing seriously at all.
>
> Many trustees and senior charity staff believe legacies are the gift of the legacy fairies, they are that complacent. They love the money flowing in but don't seem to think the flow can be promoted nor that it might stop one day without such promotion.

Adding Charity
to Your Will
or IRA

A quick guide to the pleasure and promise
of charitable bequests

Hampton Roads
Community Foundation

Inspiring Philanthropy. Changing Lives.

Note the subhead: "A quick guide to the pleasure and promise of charitable bequests." This booklet, launched in 2011, had already gone through three updates
by 2017. It helps bring in dozens of new legacy donors every year.

And they're a bargain

Lawyer and professor at Texas Tech University Russell James, America's foremost expert on legacy giving, had this to say recently:

> Among organizations receiving any gifts from wills or estates, on average organizations receive an almost 50% greater share of gift income from such gifts than the share of total fundraising they devote to such fundraising. In other words, such organizations devote 4.56% of their fundraising budgets to estate gifts, but receive 6.74% of their total gift income from estate gifts. Thus, compared to other fundraising expenditure types, fundraising devoted to estate gifts may generate a substantially larger amount of income.[15]

Translation: hunting for bequests is dirt cheap, compared to other types of fundraising.

---

15 Reported on the Bloomerang blog, https://bloomerang.co/blog/.

CHAPTER 39

Why fundraisers quit

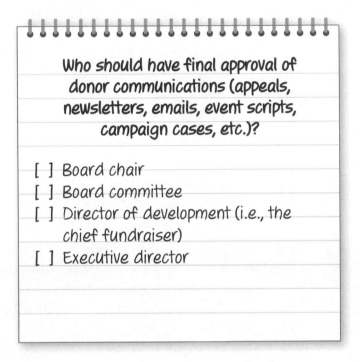

Who should have final approval of donor communications (appeals, newsletters, emails, event scripts, campaign cases, etc.)?

[ ] Board chair
[ ] Board committee
[ ] Director of development (i.e., the chief fundraiser)
[ ] Executive director

It's her neck on the line. It's her responsibility to raise the funds. You'll judge her on that bottom line.

Which means, in a responsibly managed nonprofit, only one person can exercise final approval over all fundraising and donor communications—the director of development.

Every tool she needs to complete her difficult assignment (direct mail appeals, newsletters, social media, all of it) must be under her exclusive control. Repeat: her EXCLUSIVE control . . . without the second-guessing of an untrained board or boss.

"Damage? Total, sir. It's what we call a global killer. The end of mankind. Doesn't matter where it hits, nothing would survive, not even bacteria."

This quote comes from my favorite popcorn movie of all time, *Armageddon*. The scene: a top NASA scientist brings the president of the United States swiftly up to speed on an impending calamity. Drawing a blank? Asteroid? Headed for earth? Wiped out the dinosaurs last time? Oil drillers led by Bruce Willis shot into space to stop it?

It's not the movie's wobbly science that woos me. What I love is the drama. Well, the nonprofit world is flush with drama these days, too.

The 2013 report *UnderDeveloped*[16] highlighted a growing crisis in America's fundraising profession: the turnover among development directors is high (staying in a fundraising job less than two years is typical), positions remain vacant forever, and candidates for senior positions are few and far between. The report found distrust and despair on both sides. A majority of executive directors surveyed were dissatisfied with their directors of development. A majority of fundraisers surveyed disliked their bosses.

Some of this, I believe, can be traced to second-guessing. If a chief fundraiser worries MORE about pleasing the boss or board than about the intricacies of raising money, the fundraising function cannot thrive. It would be like trying to get seeds to sprout under concrete.

---

16 Jeanne Bell and Maria Cornelius, *UnderDeveloped: A National Study of Challenges Facing Nonprofit Fundraising* (CompassPoint and the Evelyn and Walter Haas, Jr., Fund, January 2013), https://www.haasjr.org/sites/default/files/resources/UnderDeveloped_CompassPoint_HaasJrFund_January%202013_0.pdf. Accessed Dec. 4, 2018.

What's the number one complaint I hear from fundraisers worldwide? "My boss won't let me do it!" Some all-too-real examples I've collected in my travels:

- "My boss wants everything 'in his voice.' He insists on writing the appeals himself. And he's boring!"
- "The archdiocese says we shouldn't spend money on a newsletter because it shows poor stewardship of donor resources."
- "My boss told me to switch to emailed newsletters because nobody reads print anymore."
- "My boss says our donors are unique, so normal rules don't apply."
- "My boss heard me out. Then he told me, and I quote, 'Sorry. That's not how we do things here.' At least he said he was sorry."
- "The board chair said he never reads anything longer than a one-page letter, so that's what he insists on."
- "My headmaster won't let me use a P.S. in an appeal. He says it's undignified."

I call this "the Ignorance Ceiling." You have someone above you who gets to say yea or nay. And that person (boss, board member or committee) has no clue what they're talking about.

For instance: About that P.S.

What her objecting headmaster didn't know was Dr. Siegfried Vögele's research done in Munich, Germany, in the 1980s, for the direct mail industry, mentioned earlier in this book.

In that notable and pivotal research, Dr. Vögele trained cameras on ordinary people as they read direct mail letters. He discovered this: the first thing people read is the Dear Whomever salutation

("Is this for me?"). Then they *immediately* flip to the closing, to see who *signed* the letter.

Which is why Dr. Vögele dubbed the P.S. "the real first paragraph of the letter." It's a high-visibility, high-value spot where you can slip in an important message, knowing the reader's eyes are almost certain to arrive within seconds of opening the envelope.

This headmaster, though, *didn't* know Dr. Vögele's research: problem #1. Problem #2? This headmaster was over-confident in his own opinion, as we humans tend to be, neuroscientists now know.

When he negated his fundraiser's training re: Vögele and the triumphant P.S., that headmaster proved himself an ass, a fool, a nitwit, a dolt, an ignoramus and quite possibly a dismissive knave with a low opinion of women.

I'm picking on men a little bit because most of the fundraisers who complain to me are female and most of their bosses seem to be male.

The fundraiser's job

Of course members of BOTH genders eagerly practice the ugly, immature, insecure, discriminatory, bullying, dispiriting, demoralizing, disheartening, disillusioning, frustrating, soul-crushing **management flaw** of second-guessing professional staff who must bow to authority for the unassailable reason that "there's an org. chart, and I rank higher than you, so please shut up and do what I say."

The fundraiser's job is NOT to kowtow to superiors on the organization chart.

The fundraiser's real job is to know and deploy as well as she can the relevant "body of knowledge," in order to attract as much financial support as she can for the mission.

There's academic research involved. There's neuroscience and psychology involved. There's vast experience available at our fingertips, through the internet. What's NOT in fundraising's body of knowledge is anyone's uninformed opinion.

If you're a boss or board member, feel free to SUGGEST ideas, especially if your fundraiser asks for your opinion. But do not undermine your fundraiser's confidence by insisting she do what you tell her to do.

When you second-guess, you're in effect saying, "I don't trust your judgment. I suspect you're ignorant." You'll soon be searching for a new development director if that's what you exude.

Research shows that training makes you money

If you are the boss, invest in your fundraisers. Training works.

A comprehensive academic study released in 2016 by Dr. Adrian Sargeant and major gifts consultant Amy Eisenstein found that each time a fundraiser attends any competent training—conference, webinar, whatever—the charity made on average an added $37,000 in income that year.

Surprising? Not really. Conferences and webinars recruit as instructors skilled veterans with impressive track records. But those $37,000 on average results *do* assume one unpredictable thing: that charity bosses got out of the fundraiser's way and let her do exactly what the training recommended.

Final note, Dear Boss: if the stuff your fundraiser wants to send out makes you nervous, that's a *good* sign. As Jeff Brooks notes: "Good fundraising makes insiders uncomfortable. They are not the correct audience."

Here's a real-life example of what happens all too often.

An ambitious fundraiser wants to raise her game. She takes a rigorous course from top professionals to learn how to write an effective direct mail appeal. She intends to send the appeal in November 2018.

She writes a letter and shows it to her instructors, all of them direct mail veterans. They offer a few suggestions, not too much, because she's pretty much got it right.

Then she pushes her now-professionally-critiqued direct mail appeal up the nonprofit's chain of command, for final sign-off. At which point she sends out this distress signal in a private post: "I'm getting push back from management that the letter's too cheesy and sickly sweet."

The most reliable signal of ultimate success I know is this: if the executive director and board chair hate and fear what I've written, then I'm pretty sure I have a winner.

Bosses and boards: please know and accept your limitations.

Should your board impanel a "communications committee"?

No. No! HELL NO!!!

They'll try to be helpful, of course.

But giving a board committee the right to approve or reject staff work is (a) lousy governance (as board experts will tell you) and (b) worse employee relations (as human resource experts will tell you). It won't end happily.

I've said it before. I'm saying it again: *communications committees are junk.*

Expecting a local small-business owner to be "fundraising savvy" is delusional. Nor do CEOs, accountants, lawyers, engineers, professors, real estate magnates nor the socially prominent (or spouses of same) possess shocking, secret fundraising knowledge.

Yet, given a committee seat and the assignment to judge, they *will* guess. And they *will* guess wrong . . . pretty much ALL the time.[17]

---

17 Trust me on this. I'm throwing decades of experience on the table.

Their collective ignorance could cost you years of lost progress. And your fundraiser, stripped of the authority that should be hers, will quit. As will the next one. As will the next one.

If you're not getting the fundraising results you want from your communications, buy a better fundraiser. Or train the one you have to do stronger communications. But don't abandon all hope and impanel a communications committee. That's driving with two wheels in the sand.

CHAPTER 40

Repeat donors are different

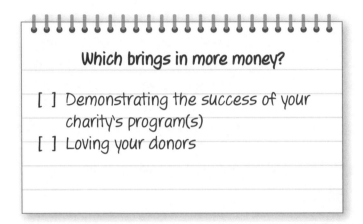

Which brings in more money?

[ ] Demonstrating the success of your
    charity's program(s)
[ ] Loving your donors

I pay attention to what interests me. And what interests me most is me. Ask anyone.

Most charities I encounter get this notion exactly backwards. They assume that it's critically important to explain how great their programs are, as a precursor to giving. And it's not a wrong assumption, exactly. As a donor, I *do* have to trust you.

But it's an insufficient assumption. As researcher Dr. Adrian Sargeant wrote in January 2016, "Once donors are in a relationship with a charity, their focus shifts from what the charity does for its beneficiaries . . . to how the relationship makes them feel (during retention/stewardship)."

Love your donors, and they'll love you back.

The shocking true story of a 1,000 percent leap in donations

The following is a striking example of how much more money you can make by switching from "organization-centric" to "donor-centric" communications.

In 2008, the foundation at Gillette Children's hospital in St. Paul, Minnesota, changed just a few things in its print donor newsletter.

The newsletter was mailed quarterly to about twenty thousand addresses. And for years, it had lost serious money, racking up an annual net loss of $40,000. With every issue mailed, a mere $5,000 came back in gifts, not enough to cover printing and postage, much less staff time.

This was a typical front-page headline, focused on how great the medicine is:

And then the foundation tried something different, mailed to the very same folks.

The team followed the Domain Formula to a T. And although the hospital's world-class medicine still made appearances in the articles, the headlines were reserved for thanking and admiring the donors. Instead of being institutional in tone, the newsletter got warm and personal. The word *you* appeared everywhere.

This was the new front-page headline, focused on making donors feel good:

Zawadi Says, "Thank You!"

You Helped a Tanzanian Girl Stand Tall on Her Own Two Feet

To meet Zawadi Rajabu, 6, is to experience gratitude through the eyes of a child. She greets you with a warm hug, a bright smile, and an emphatic, "Thank you!" Before you can grasp why you deserve such adoration, you catch a mischievous glint in her eye. "No catch me!" she taunts, running in the opposite direction. Another game of tag has begun, and —

needed a surgeon trained in the Ilizarov method — a complex technique for reshaping bones, developed by Gavriil Ilizarov, M.D., in a remote Siberian hospital. It was a tall order, to be sure.

But a Google search quickly uncovered one of the few surgeons in the world who could help Zawadi: Mark Dahl, M.D., pediatric orthopaedic surgeon at Gillette Children's Specialty

It was a risky experiment with many internal doubters. What happened?

Between one issue and the next, giving prompted by the news-letter soared 1,000 percent.

Instead of receiving the usual $5,000 per issue, the Gillette foundation saw $50,000 come back in the mail thanks to its new approach.

And that wasn't a one-time spike, either: revenue remained at the $50,000 level every issue . . . as long as the foundation kept the focus on the donor and didn't slip back into its old, institutional ways. I checked again late in 2017: Gillette's print newsletter was still a moneymaker.

As best-selling marketing expert Seth Godin insists: "The story's about the donor." He points out that "every time someone donates to a good cause, they're buying a story, a story that's worth more than the amount they donated. It might be the story of doing the right thing, or fitting in, or pleasing a friend or honoring a memory, but the story has value. For many, it's the story of what it means to be part of a community."

Outro

Fundraising is sales. The donor is your customer.

Jerry Cianciolo, my editor, asked me to write a closing statement. He even suggested a question: "What has startled YOU the most about the fundraising profession over the past years?"

That's easy, Jerry.

I asked of fundraisers: *Who* is *your customer?* And they didn't have a ready answer.

"That's odd"

When I got into charity work, I'd already done twenty years as a sales copywriter. I'd trained and trained and trained. And I'd written sales materials for stuff and services ranging from online lottery systems to super-luxury yachts to adult education to disability insurance.

They were all the same, in one sense: they knew and cared about their customers.

In sales, you *revere* the customer. You *study* the customer. You *survey* customers, hoping to get inside their heads as much as you can. You learn what they *want* . . . what they *need* . . . and you're very aware of their numerous emotional triggers (including fears and hopes).

It can be a pressure-cooker line of work. After all, if you don't make sales, you're fired.

I liked that part. It was competitive. And my stuff worked.

In sales, the goal is clear: to have your product/service accepted into a person's life . . . into that person's daily story . . . into that person's sometimes fragile, sometimes steel-hard, self-image.

Back to fundraising: viewed technically, without whitewash or

173

halos, fundraising is just a type of sales. You make an offer. People buy. (Though mostly they *don't* buy: neither commercial wares nor nonprofit offers.)

So what *startled* me, Jerry? As a copywriter attempting to raise money for charity, I knew I was in sales. Yet I had no idea who the customer was. And the fundraisers who were my clients didn't seem to know either.

It took me years to rustle up any kind of satisfactory answer.

Eventually, though, the pieces—for me, anyway—fell in place. Finally I realized that fundraising's core "customer" was simply the donor. And those customers hope to buy something important.

What you sell when you don't sell shoes or food

MarketSmart is a Maryland-based agency that helps charities with bequest marketing and other major giving campaigns. Its success has been nothing short of amazing. In 2018, Greg Warner, CEO, shared his personal understanding of "Why People Give to Charity":

- A chance to be moved by someone's story in an emotional way

- An opportunity to feel I'm not powerless in the face of need

- Empowerment to feel that I'm changing someone's life

- A sense of closeness to a community or group

- A possible tax deduction

- A way to memorialize someone

- A way to continue my family tradition since I was raised to give to charity

- A chance to be "hip" by supporting a charity

- A way to feel connected to other people

- A chance to be the "hero"

- An opportunity to leave a legacy that perpetuates me, my ideals or my cause

- An opportunity to give something back to others

- A way to follow my religion

- I want to be seen as a leader/role model

That's a pretty exhaustive list from a well-informed frontline fundraising practitioner.

As a frequent donor myself, reflecting on my own reasons for giving, I now believe that what charities mostly sell to individuals is meaning and feelings. Among other things:

- Purpose. ("I did a good thing.")

- A way to reciprocate. ("I want to give back.")

- A sense of self. ("I was brought up to be helpful.")

- A sense of place and belonging. ("I did my bit for my community.")

- Emotional gratification. ("Giving feels good.")

- Reassurance and relief . . . ("I *am* a decent person!")

- . . . especially to the aging. ("I'm NOT useless!")

To your donors, these "meaningful" things, these intensely *felt* things, are worth a lot more than "stuff." (Though the occasional tote bag or T-shirt showing the world my values . . . well, that can be nice, too.)

"Fundraising isn't about money," the great Harold Sumption said in 1977, "it's about work that urgently needs doing."[18]

Donors need to feel that they are an important part of that work that urgently needs doing. That's the primary job of all donor communications: to make "me, the donor" feel useful, proud of myself and wanted.

Do that job well . . . and your fundraising worries are over.

---

18 Who is Harold Sumption? He's a British advertising superstar who, as a volunteer, guided the messaging that helped turn the tiny Oxford Committee for Famine Relief (founded 1942) into the international doing-good powerhouse we know today, working in more than ninety countries.

The answers

CHAPTER 1

How old is the typical US donor?

[ ] 35 years of age
[ ] 50 years of age
[X] 75 years of age

CHAPTER 2

How big should the type be?

[ ] 10 pt.
[ ] 12 pt.
[X] 14 pt.

CHAPTER 3

"People over 70 are still developing."

[X] True
[ ] False

CHAPTER 4

When you make a donation, how many "happiness chemicals" does your brain release?

[ ] None
[X] Three
[ ] Six

CHAPTER 5

Do humans react negatively to false flattery?

[X] No
[ ] Yes

CHAPTER 6

How long does the average donor stick around?

[ ] 1–3 years
[X] 4–6 years [annual giver]
[X] 7–10 years [monthly giver]
[ ] more than 10 years

CHAPTER 7

How quickly should you thank a first-time donor?

[X] Within 48 hours
[ ] Within a week
[ ] Within a month

CHAPTER 8

Should you include an "ask" in your thank-you letter?

[ ] Always
[ ] Never
[X] Dealer's choice

CHAPTER 9

Is direct mail past its prime?

[ ] Yes
[X] No

CHAPTER 10

What's a successful response rate for a donor-acquisition appeal?

[ ] 15% (you mail 100, you get 15 gifts back)

[ ] 8% (you mail 100, you get eight gifts back)

[X] 1% (you mail 100, you get one gift back)

CHAPTER 11

How often in a single appeal can you ask for a gift?

[ ] Once is enough

[ ] Three or four times is OK

[X] Sky's the limit

CHAPTER 12

Are fundraising events important to a charity's success?

[ ] Yes

[X] No

[ ] Maybe

CHAPTER 13

What percentage of US charitable income is now raised online?

[ ] More than 25% of the total

[ ] Somewhere between 10–25% of the total

[X] Less than 10% of the total [2017 data]

CHAPTER 14

What's the best length for a direct mail letter?

[ ] 1 page

[ ] 2 pages

[X] 4 pages

CHAPTER 15

What's the preferred "grade level" for a direct mail appeal?

[X] 6th grade

[ ] 9th grade

[ ] 12th grade

CHAPTER 16

Should you indent paragraphs in an appeal letter?

[X] Yes

[ ] No

CHAPTER 17

What is the purpose of an envelope?

[X] To get opened

[ ] To protect the contents

CHAPTER 18

Which match ratio brings in the most money?

[X] 1 for 1 (i.e., each donated dollar is matched with a second dollar from another source; so your $1 gift buys $2 worth of impact)

[ ] 2 for 1 (your $1 gift equals $3 worth of impact)

[ ] 3 for 1 (your $1 gift equals $4 worth of impact)

CHAPTER 19

How often can you ask in a year without driving off donors?

[ ] Once a year

[ ] Three times a year

[ ] A dozen times a year

[X] 21 times year

CHAPTER 20

If you "raise awareness" in your community, you'll raise more money.

[ ] Yes

[ ] No

[X] Maybe

CHAPTER 21

How many charities will a typical donor give to each year?

[ ] 1 to 4

[X] 5 or more

CHAPTER 22

How big is a typical first gift in the US?

[ ] $15

[X] $45

[ ] $135

CHAPTER 23

Which is better?

[ ] A single annual gift of $120

[X] A gift of $10 every month (= $120 in a year)

CHAPTER 24

What is the leading cause of donor attrition?

[ ] Charity admitted to a financial setback

[X] Donor wonders, "Did my gift make a difference?"

[ ] Fundraising costs are too high

CHAPTER 25

Which format is better?

[ ] Digital newsletter

[X] Print newsletter

CHAPTER 26

Print newsletters can make as much money as direct mail appeals.

[ ] False

[X] True

CHAPTER 27

Which is more convincing?

[ ] Stats

[ ] Stories

[X] Depends on your target audience

CHAPTER 28

"We need to educate our donors."

[ ] True
[X] False

CHAPTER 29

For an animal welfare charity, which will raise more money?

[ ] Stories of animal rescues and adoptions
[X] Stories of cruelty to animals

CHAPTER 30

Which will raise more money?

[ ] Picture of a happy child
[X] Picture of a sad child

CHAPTER 31

Which has the longer attention span?

[X] A goldfish
[ ] The average adult American

CHAPTER 32

Which pronoun raises more money?

[ ] We
[X] You

CHAPTER 33

Which generation consumes the most online content?

[ ] Generation Y/Millennials/Born 1981–2000
[ ] Generation X/Born 1965–1980
[X] Baby Boomers/Born 1946–1964
[ ] Mature/Silents/Born 1927–1945

CHAPTER 34

Which sequence of gift amounts raised the most?

[X] Smallest to largest: $50, $100, $250
[ ] Largest to smallest: $250, $100, $50

CHAPTER 35

Should we start with a letter from the boss?

[ ] Yes
[X] No
[ ] Maybe

CHAPTER 36

Where does most US charity come from?

[ ] Corporations
[ ] Foundations
[X] Individuals

CHAPTER 37

Which is your biggest unexploited fundraising opportunity?

[X] Charitable bequests

[ ] Facebook fundraising

[ ] Major gifts

CHAPTER 38

Where do most charitable bequests come from?

[X] Mid-class estates (probating at $2 million or less)

[ ] Wealthier estates (probating at more than $2 million)

CHAPTER 39

Who should have final approval of donor communications (appeals, newsletters, emails, event scripts, campaign cases, etc.)?

[ ] Board chair

[ ] Board committee

[X] Director of development (i.e., the chief fundraiser)

[ ] Executive director

CHAPTER 40

Which brings in more money?

[ ] Demonstrating the success of your charity's program(s)

[X] Loving your donors

Contributors

Contributors to this book, in one way or another, witting or not, living or never-to-be-forgotten, include an international gang of experts, stars, voyagers and incidents:

Agents of Good ~ AIGA ~ Tobin Aldrich ~ Angel Aloma ~ American Marketing Association ~ Tad Ames ~ Caoileann Appleby ~ Ron Arena ~ Armageddon (movie) ~ Ask Direct ~ AS220 ~ Association of Fundraising Professionals ~ Claire Axelrad ~ Bob Ball ~ Beth Beall ~ Antoine Bechara ~ Ashley Belanger ~ The Better Fundraising Co. ~ Blackbaud ~ Bloomerang ~ Bluefrog ~ Pat and Sue Bradley ~ Kathy Brennan ~ Michelle Brinson ~ Jeff Brooks ~ Ken Burnett ~ BuzzStream ~ Donald B. Calne ~ John Caples ~ Dale Carnegie ~ Denisa Casement ~ The Case Writers ~ CFRE ~ Chronicle of Philanthropy ~ Robert Cialdini ~ Jerry Cianciolo ~ Tina Cincotti ~ Alan Clayton ~ Catherine Clifford ~ Maggie Cohn ~ Sandie Collette ~ CompassPoint ~ Connecticut Forest & Park Association ~ Crisis Aid ~ Lisa Cron ~ Roger Craver ~ Stephanie and Chris Davenport ~ Harriet Day ~ Fabienne DeSoza ~ The Domain Group ~ DonorVoice ~ Roger Dooley ~ Shanon Doolittle ~ Peter Drury ~ Julie Edwards ~ Amy Eisenstein ~ Tony Elischer ~ Ted Elliott ~ Emerson & Church ~ eNonprofits Benchmarks Study ~ Entrepreneur ~ Leah Eustace ~ Fast Company ~ First World War ~ Rudolf Flesch ~ Shell Folder ~ Food for the Poor ~ Fractl ~ Friends of the Mississippi River ~ Future Fundraising Now ~ Lynn Gaertner-Johnston ~ Gayle Gifford ~ Gillette Children's ~ Giving Tuesday ~ Giving USA ~ Seth Godin ~ Good Works ~ Fraser Green ~ Rory Green ~ Sheena Greer ~ Chip Grizzard ~ Pam Grow ~ Johannes Gutenberg ~ The Evelyn and Walter Haas, Jr., Fund ~ Ann Hale ~ Hampton Roads Community Foundation ~ Sally Kirby

Hartman ~ John Haydon ~ Dan Hill ~ Andrea Hopkins ~ Jon Howard ~ Cory J. Howat ~ Humane Society of Northeast Georgia ~ Jerry Huntsinger ~ IFC ~ Russell James ~ Andrée Joyaux ~ Simone Joyaux ~ Daniel Kahneman ~ Dean Karlan ~ Andrea Kihlstedt ~ J. Peter Kincaid ~ Joseph LeDoux ~ John Lepp ~ Richard C. Levin ~ Abraham Lincoln (his Gettysburg Address being a brilliant case for support) ~ John List ~ Jim Little ~ Beth Ann Locke ~ Lollypop Farm ~ Chuck Longfield ~ David Love ~ Jay Love ~ Jen Love ~ love generally ~ Linda Lysakowski ~ MarketSmart ~ Masterworks ~ McConkey Johnston International UK (now the Christian Fundraising Consultancy) ~ Ruth McDonald ~ Mike McKenna ~ Harvey McKinnon ~ Kivi Leroux Miller ~ MoonClerk ~ The Motley Fool ~ National Council for Aging Care ~ The New York Times ~ Stephen Nill ~ The Nonprofit Storytelling Conference ~ The Nonprofit Times ~ Norges Blindeforbund ~ North Carolina State University ~ npENGAGE ~ Damian O'Broin ~ David Ogilvy ~ Jerry Panas ~ Pareto ~ Ben Paynter ~ PBS TV ~ Amanda Pearce ~ Sophie Penney ~ Richard Perry ~ The Philanthropy Centre ~ The Philanthropy Roundtable ~ Mark Phillips ~ Stephen Pidgeon ~ Marc Pitman ~ Stephen G. Post ~ Psychology Today ~ Richard Radcliffe ~ Terry Rossio ~ Jim Sardina ~ Adrian Sargeant ~ Lisa Sargent ~ Patti Saunders ~ Eric Schmidt ~ Jeff Schreifels ~ Kevin Schulman ~ Nancy Schwartz ~ Rick Schwartz ~ Steven Screen ~ Sea Change ~ Jen Shang ~ Alan Sharpe ~ Sharp HealthCare ~ Steven Shattuck ~ Matthew Sherrington ~ Showcase of Fundraising Innovation and Inspiration (SOFII) ~ Emily Silak ~ Paul Slovic ~ George Smith ~ David Solie ~ Christiana Stergiou ~ Stephen Stills ~ Marty Stone ~ David Stout ~ Ilene Strizver ~ Tom Struthers ~ Tom Suddes ~ Target Analytics Group ~ Steve Thomas ~ Sean Triner ~ Joseph Troncale ~ Mark Twain ~ Amos Tversky ~ USC Annenberg ~ Jose van Herpt ~ Veritus Group ~ Vida Joven ~ Patricia Vidov ~ Siegfried Vögele ~ Erica Waasdorp ~ Keith & Rosmarie Waldrop ~ Greg Warner ~ Mal Warwick ~ Jerry Weissman ~ Colin Wheildon ~ The Whiny Donor ~ White Lion Press ~ Wikipedia ~ Paul J. Zak ~ Hermann Zapf

About the Author

The New York Times recently called Tom Ahern "one of the country's most sought-after creators of fund-raising messages." He specializes in applying the discoveries of psychology and neuroscience to the day-to-day business of attracting and retaining donors. He's authored six well-received books; his latest is *What Your Donors Want . . . and Why!* Each year, Tom teaches thousands of fund-raisers internationally about donor communications through conferences (in 2018: Italy, Norway, dozens of North American locations), webinars and online courses. Included amongst his audit and training clients: ADRA, Boys & Girls Clubs of America, Chabad on Campus, Christus Health, the Connecticut Humane Society, Presbyterian Villages of Michigan, Save the Children Global, Sharp Healthcare (San Diego), USA for UNHCR and Waypoint Adventures.

Copies of this and other books from the publisher are available at discount when purchased in quantity for boards of directors or staff. Call 508-359-0019 or visit www.emersonandchurch.com.

Emerson
& Church
PUBLISHERS

15 Brook Street—Medfield, MA 02052
Tel. 508-359-0019
www.emersonandchurch.com